'Lendvai draws on his vast experience and clear, crisp prose to skewer the naïve, duplicitous and hypocritical politicians of our age. He is a shining beacon for anybody who cares about democracy and truth.'

Misha Glenny, author of *McMafia* and *The Fall of Yugoslavia*

'A major reckoning with Western Europe's policies towards Vladimir Putin ... [There is] recognisable emotion behind [Lendvai's] analysis—densely packed with facts, figures and quotes ... Why did it take so long for the West to understand the true nature of Putinism? Lendvai reaches far into the past in search of answers ... he shows ... the world as it is.'

Süddeutsche Zeitung

'Lendvai has a rare journalistic gift: not only can he analyse a situation, but he can tell a story. After decades of brilliant foreign policy journalism, he vividly describes his many experiences ... showing their significance in context ... Why were so many Western politicians and intellectuals, from left and right, so mistaken about the nature of the Russian regime, and especially Putin? Lendvai provides a profound explanation ... The chapter on ... the Yugoslav state collapse is ... well worth reading—and a treat for those who worshipped Sebastian Kurz.'

Der Standard (Austria)

'Lendvai doesn't just castigate political parties; he also takes aim at ... leading businesses ... [in] his panorama of hypocrisy ... Lendvai has no remedy. Nevertheless, he is ... a [seasoned] traveller of the turbulent twentieth century, [who] knows that people want to be deceived. This was already the case in 1580, when Montaigne wrote: "What we call truth today is not what is true, but what one can persuade others to believe."'

Neue Zürcher Zeitung

BLIND-SPOT POLITICS

PAUL LENDVAI

Blind-Spot Politics

*Appeasement, Authoritarianism
and Hypocrisy in Europe*

HURST & COMPANY, LONDON

First published in the United Kingdom in 2025 by
C. Hurst & Co. (Publishers) Ltd.,
New Wing, Somerset House, Strand, London, WC2R 1LA
© Paul Lendvai, 2025
All rights reserved.

Distributed in the United States, Canada and Latin America by
Oxford University Press, 198 Madison Avenue, New York, NY 10016,
United States of America.

The right of Paul Lendvai to be identified as the author of
this publication is asserted by him in accordance with the
Copyright, Designs and Patents Act, 1988.

A Cataloguing-in-Publication data record for this book
is available from the British Library.

ISBN: 9781805264286

www.hurstpublishers.com

Printed and bound in Great Britain by Bell & Bain Ltd, Glasgow

CONTENTS

CONTENTS

PREFACE

Mundus vult decipi, ergo decipiatur.

(The world wants to be deceived, so let it be deceived.)

"He has obviously deceived everyone," said the Social Democratic prime minister of Mecklenburg–Western Pomerania, Manuela Schwesig, to explain why the state government she led was closely linked to Putin's Russia until the Russian invasion of Ukraine, completing the controversial Nord Stream 2 pipeline with the help of a dubious foundation.[1] Why was not only she, but also numerous German and Austrian, French and American politicians and opinion makers, so often and for so long wrong in their assessment of Russian policy? Why did it take so long for the institutions of the European Union (EU) to find the right answers to the authoritarian developments in Hungary and Poland? Why were they so long and so late to recognise the danger posed by nationalist autocrats to the liberal values of the West?

As the title of this book suggests, I would like to focus in particular on the role of hypocrisy, double standards, human and political duplicity in the actions and statements of top politicians, which in retrospect are incomprehensible. The politics of the past decades have maintained the illusion that the attraction of democracy is irresistible, leaving deceivers triumphant from Moscow to Budapest and the victims self-satisfied from Berlin to Vienna.

The philosopher of scepticism, Michel de Montaigne, wrote in 1580: "The art of dissimulation is counted among the most excellent qualities of the century," and he added: "What we call truth today is not what is true, but what one can persuade others to believe."[2]

In this book, I would also like to combine my personal experiences as a commentator and reporter in global political crisis situations with the flood of new information on the blunders and misinterpretations of Western politics in order to expose the obfuscation and the fraud. I will therefore begin with my personal, random and yet highly symbolic encounters with "victims" and "perpetrators", with personalities from Russian society who operate behind a mask and to whom Nietzsche's words apply: "The apparent world is the only one, the 'true world' is only a lie."[3]

What follows is a look at the forerunners of those who today "understand" Putin and Orbán—those famous intellectuals, authors and reporters who as "political pilgrims" had praised dictators from Stalin to Castro, whether out of naivety or financial interests. In two chapters I describe the co-responsibility of those German politicians, above all former chancellor Gerhard Schröder, who played down, legitimised and indirectly co-financed the Putin regime.

An important part of the book is the policy of appeasement, coupled with hypocrisy, towards the past and present arsonists in the Balkans, where from Serbia to Kosovo, from Bosnia to Macedonia, time bombs are still ticking. As for EU enlargement by the accession of the Balkan states, hypocrisy continues to characterise the attitude of both sides: "Some act as if they want to enlarge, others act as if they want to join."[4]

Hungarian prime minister Viktor Orbán, who has ruled Hungary unchallenged since 2010, can only be portrayed as the world champion of political hypocrisy, as the ruler of a mafia state disguised as an "illiberal democracy", with deplorable consequences for European politics. To him, above all, the insight of Montaigne applies: "Hypocrites are admirably adept at speaking out against hypocrisy. Whoever thinks he has an advantage in this, even if he spends a great deal of time doing so, only continues to pursue the cause of masks: he himself remains a masked personality."[5]

In a subsequent chapter I describe his Hungarian-American counterpart George Soros, once admired as a philanthropist but now depicted worldwide as a hated demon by the threatened autocrats, as a victim of the global success of conspiracy theories.

The final chapter is devoted to Austria, where, according to Thomas Bernhard, "mendacity is at home",[6] where shining dazzlers, from Jörg Haider to Sebastian Kurz, have made masquerade and duplicity the general rule in politics and thus achieved "miracles of blind and boundless compliance of the people".[7]

1

VIOLENCE AND RESISTANCE

ENCOUNTERS WITH ACTORS OF
RUSSIAN POLITICS

The actors leave the stage after they have played their part.

Stanisław Jerzy Lec

My first and almost certainly last personal encounter with President Vladimir Putin of Russia took place on the occasion of his first official state visit to Austria on 9 February 2001. Federal President Thomas Klestil hosted a glittering state banquet in the Hofburg in honour of the Russian guest. Beforehand, the Austrian guests were formally introduced to him. Our meeting—Putin acknowledged my platitudes in Russian with a friendly smile—was also captured by a photographer, with the photo reprinted in my autobiography.

The only vivid memory I have of that dinner is of my right-hand neighbour. Today, many years later, I regret the missed opportunity of a longer conversation with this friendly, attractive woman. Her name was Lyudmila Narusova Sobchak. I knew that she was the widow of Anatoly Sobchak, the first freely elected mayor of St Petersburg (1991–1996). Our conversation in a mixture of broken English and Russian lasted only a few minutes. I was soon embroiled in a lively chat with my Austrian neighbours across the table and to my left about the tensions between Thomas Klestil and Chancellor Wolfgang Schüssel at the time, and neglected her almost completely.

At the time, however, I had no idea of the suspicious circumstances surrounding Sobchak's death and the allegations of corruption against him and his then deputy, Vladimir Putin.[1] He died a year before the banquet at the Hofburg, and the presence of his widow in the Russian delegation was proof of her close relationship with President Putin. Narusova was a member of parliament and later became a long-standing member of the Russian Federation Council. The friendly contacts with Putin dated back to the Soviet era, when Anatoly Sobchak was a professor of law at Leningrad University. Putin and his successor as interim president, Dmitry Medvedev, were among his students. A description of Sobchak's political rise and fall is beyond the scope of this book. What is certain, however, is that in a BBC interview almost twenty years later, Narusova publicly confirmed the rumours about her husband's death. When asked by the reporter whether her husband had been murdered, she said after some hesitation: "I don't know."[2]

After the start of the Russian war of aggression against Ukraine, she stirred up interest several times with her critical statements. She was, for example, the only one of the 170 members of the Federation Council (the actual upper house of parliament) to abstain from voting in mid-April 2023 on the digitalisation of conscription into the army. Without criticising Putin by name, she justified her critical stance by means of her husband's legacy in an unusual interview with the newspaper *Novaya Gazeta Europe*, which is published in Russian and English in Latvia.[3]

Shocking murders

By a chain of coincidences, I have also met several other Russian personalities, before their rise or after their fall, who appeared in St Petersburg or Moscow as opponents or helpers of Putin on his path to absolute power. Even brief acquaintances offer the chronicler personal clues to the fate of these people. The following story also took place in St Petersburg two years before Sobchak's death. In the late 1990s, Russian newspapers called St Petersburg, once built by Tsar Peter the Great as a "window to the West", the "capital of crime". In the course of clashes between political groups, some with links to mafia gangs, attacks on politicians, businessmen and critical journalists were part of everyday life. The murder of Galina Starovoitova, member of parliament and leader of the "Democratic Russia" movement, on 20 November 1998, caused the greatest sensation and aroused intense sympathy. Two assassins lay in wait for her in the stairwell to her apartment in St Petersburg and shot her three times in the head with a machine gun at around 11 pm. She died on the spot.

In her groundbreaking analysis of the Putin regime, *Putin's Web*, Catherine Belton emphasises that Starovoitova was murdered because of her investigation of local corruption only four months after Putin's appointment as head of the domestic intelligence service: "She was the leading democrat in Saint Petersburg and the loudest voice against corruption. After her death, the city fell into deep mourning and the whole country was in shock."[4] According to Belton, former colleagues and one of her best friends were convinced that she had been murdered on the orders of the St Petersburg security authorities linked to corruption networks that were being investigated by her.

I was shocked when the news was reported because I had known Galina well. We had both attended the fortieth general assembly of the International Press Institute in Kyoto (21–24 April 1991). She attracted attention right from the start with her outspoken statements. In contrast to the more reserved Alexander Yakovlev, the closest advisor to Soviet President Mikhail Gorbachev, who was also present, she sharply criticised the opponents of reform in Moscow.

The political career of Galina Starovoitova began with her election as representative of the Armenian Republic in the Soviet Congress of People's Deputies; she was also a member of the first opposition parliamentary group, which included the civil rights activist and Nobel Peace Prize winner Andrei Sakharov. She described herself as the daughter of "a proud Cossack" and a "Russified Belarusian". Sensitised by her family history, she published more than seventy studies about the peoples of the Caucasus. At the conference in Kyoto, she passionately condemned the oppression of minorities and the anti-Semitic tendencies in the Soviet system, and spoke from personal experience about the problems of ethnic minorities in the Caucasus and the danger of Russian nationalism. During our one-on-one talks, she was even more outspoken and made no secret of her concerns about the offensive of the opponents of reform.

In January 1991, despite warnings from the military, she led a huge demonstration in Moscow with hundreds of thousands of participants under the slogan "Freedom for Lithuania!" The first head of state of a free Lithuania, Vytautas Landsbergis, highlighted Galina's courage by quoting her: "If men are cowards, then a woman must lead the way."[5]

Four months after our meeting in Kyoto, the world witnessed the failed coup against Gorbachev and the rise of Boris Yeltsin to the presidency of the Russian Federation. Starovoitova became Yeltsin's advisor for national minorities. She was dismissed at the end of 1992 because of her criticism of government policy in the conflict with the Ossetians and Ingush. She spoke out openly against Yeltsin's Chechnya policy and called for the punishment of crimes against humanity in Nagorno-Karabakh (in Azerbaijan) and Chechnya.

During this turbulent time, she came to Vienna for a lecture and contacted me. We met at Café Griensteidl to talk, and she reported on the escalation of political tensions and death threats after her appearances on television. At least she had managed to get her son a scholarship to a university in London. She sounded determined and also told me that she would soon be delivering lectures at Brown University in Providence, Rhode Island, on the politics of self-determination for ethnic minorities. Since I had lectured on the political situation in the Balkans at the same university a few months earlier, she could also give my name as a reference before being granted the status of visiting professor for several years.

Nevertheless she remained active in Russian politics and was elected chairwoman of the Democratic Russia movement in 1998. She was to prepare and lead the alliance in the parliamentary elections in December 1998. During the campaign, she criticised the expansion of the powers of the FSB, the domestic secret service, and voted against the nomination of Yevgeny Primakov as prime minister. Galina Starovoitova was a promising candidate for the post of governor of the Petrograd region and was even considered in the media as a potential presidential candidate. She had to die because she knew too much about the corrupt scene in St Petersburg and the political links to the *siloviki* (the representatives of the secret services and the military in important political and economic positions).[6]

Five years after my meeting with Galina Starovoitova, I was asked in 1996 to act as host and moderator at a working lunch for Boris Nemtsov, governor of the Russian province of Nizhny Novgorod on the occasion of a Central and Eastern European Economic Summit organised by the Davos World Economic Forum in Salzburg. The meeting with the young governor aroused particular interest among foreign journalists and entrepreneurs. They wanted to know why the region—roughly the size of Austria, with a population of three and a half million—had become a role model for the whole of Russia. The guest, then in his mid-thirties, explained in fluent English, sometimes with a smile, how he had taken action against the old, corrupt nomenklatura since 1991, how he had brought in foreign consultants and tried to break the power of the monopolies by promoting private initiatives.

Although the three-day event was attended by dozens of presidents, heads of government and ministers,

Nemtsov was considered one of the stars. Klaus Schwab, the founder and president of the World Economic Forum, had already included him in 1993 as the first Russian in the group of "future world leaders". Both the audience who crowded around the chairs at our dinner or listened standing up and the audience at a discussion round with Nemtsov the following day were captivated by his openness and direct style. He repeatedly emphasised that the most difficult part of implementing far-reaching liberal economic reforms, privatising state-owned enterprises, agriculture and trade in Russia, had been changing people's mentality and finding people to assume responsibility.

Nemtsov was an extraordinary personality, talented and handsome, yet at the same time modest and likeable. In the years that followed, he became extremely popular beyond the region, was re-elected as governor and in 1997 was appointed one of two first deputy prime ministers by President Boris Yeltsin. "I will not lie, I will not steal and I will not take bribes," he said when he took office. With 50 per cent of the vote in opinion polls, he appeared to be a promising candidate for election as Russian president after leaving the government. However, "the family", that is, the closest circle around the seriously ill and discredited Boris Yeltsin, opted for Vladimir Putin. The consequences of his election as president in March 2000 are well known.

Boris Nemtsov warned of the impending dangers of a dictatorship as early as January 2004 in an article in the newspaper *Nezavisimaya Gazeta* entitled "On the Danger of Putinism", written with his advisor and friend Vladimir Kara-Murza.[7] Nemtsov spoke out against the Putin regime with the same courage and passion that he had shown as governor and minister in pushing forward the reform measures. On 10 December 2014, he gave an outspoken interview to ARD, the German television channel: "Russia is a classic mafia state with the 'mafioso' Putin at the top. There is a tight circle of people who are fed by this mafioso and are completely dependent on him. No laws apply to them. They control all the mass media. Putin sees enemies everywhere. This is at the level of paranoia [...] Sanctions [because of the annexation of Crimea] against the Russian people are bad. Sanctions against the scumbags, scoundrels and bandits from Putin's entourage who have become billionaires are good. You can't make any compromises with Putin. He has taken Crimea. Next he will take Kiev, then Moldova, then Poland and the Baltic states. He is a robber, who only understands the language of strength, no other language."[8]

Ten weeks later, Boris Nemtsov, 55, was dead. He was killed by four shots to the back and to the head on the Moskva Bridge, accompanied by his unharmed girlfriend, within sight of the Kremlin on the evening of 27 February 2015.

As in other political murder cases, the alleged perpetrators were sentenced to prison, but the names of those who had ordered the murder remain unknown to this day. Nemtsov's eldest daughter, who lives abroad, the European Parliament and the Council of Europe have so far called in vain for an international investigation.[9]

Galina Starovoitova and Boris Nemtsov are unforgettable for me. Their fate confirms what Arthur Koestler wrote in early 1944 about the mass murder of the Jews and what also applies to understanding the numbers of victims of Stalin's purges or Putin's waves of arrests during the protests against the war in Ukraine: "Statistics don't bleed, it's the detail that counts."[10] That is why even brief but intense personal acquaintances with people who suffer tragic individual fates have an incomparably greater impact than long treatises with precise numbers of victims on the same subject.

The perpetrators

In a long life, one comes into contact with future victims of dictatorships as well as with "perpetrators", that is, the representatives of an authoritarian system or even a dictatorship. So it happened that I—who had never had anything to do with secret services—got to know two heads of the Russian secret service. In the fall of 1986, an article by Yevgeny Primakov on Soviet foreign policy appeared in the *Europäische Rundschau*, a quarterly journal which I edited, under the title "Philosophy of Security". Primakov was then director of the Institute for World Economy and International Relations in Moscow.

His essay, distributed by the Novosti press agency, contained no new ideas and merely repeated the central points of the foreign policy announced by General Secretary Mikhail Gorbachev at the 27th Party Congress.

I never thought that the author, described as a journalist and Middle East expert of many years' standing, would in the following years become a member of the Politburo of the Soviet Communist Party (CPSU) and head of the foreign intelligence service. Obviously, he was already a high-ranking intelligence officer as *Pravda*'s Middle East correspondent. I met him personally in the turbulent period before the collapse of the Soviet Union, when he was already a candidate for the Politburo, on the fringes of a conference of the International Press Institute. I remember that during a background discussion he still took a hard line regarding the aspirations for independence of the Baltic Soviet republics.

Nothing could better illustrate the later relaxation in the Gorbachev era than the following incident. In 1995, I took the liberty of asking the Austrian ambassador in Moscow to transmit to Primakov—then head of the foreign intelligence service—a personal letter. In it, I reminded him of his article and of our meeting, and then, with reference to the policy of glasnost (openness), impudently asked for information concerning me from the KGB archives. The reason was the preparation of my autobiography. In a polite letter, the press officer of the foreign secret service told me that I was only mentioned in the joint archive of the state security services of the former socialist countries as a "person suspected of having contacts with the West German secret service".[11]

Of course, this was just as much nonsense as the colourful lies in the Hungarian and Czechoslovakian files, but it was remarkable that Moscow reacted at all. Primakov became foreign minister in 1996 and was even prime minister in 1998–1999, before Yeltsin and the "family" appointed Putin as his successor. In 2007, Primakov, a lifelong hardliner and Putin's companion, was awarded the Grand Decoration of Honour in Gold on Ribbon for services to the Republic of Austria, services that are completely unknown to me.

My journey to meet Vladimir Kryuchkov, who played an important role in Hungarian and Soviet history, was more exciting and more costly. In preparation for my book on the Hungarian uprising in October 1956, I managed, with the help of the Austrian ambassador in Moscow, to make contact with a former member of the secret service who was prepared to arrange an interview, for a handsome fee, with the former KGB chief General Vladimir Kryuchkov in his apartment.[12] It took place on 26 September 2005. Kryuchkov served as third secretary in the Soviet embassy in Budapest from 1954 to 1957 and became the closest collaborator of Ambassador Yuri Andropov. He later was in charge of Hungarian affairs as an official of the Central Committee of the CPSU. He was actively involved in the suppression of the Hungarian uprising in 1956.

During our conversation, conducted partly in Hungarian, partly translated from Russian, we primarily discussed the role of the Communist Party leader János Kádár (1956–1988) and that of the prime minister during the uprising, Imre Nagy, who was executed in 1958 following a secret trial.

Kryuchkov became Andropov's bureau chief when he took over the leadership of the KGB in 1967 and rose to the rank of army general in 1988. He was a key figure in the failed conspiracy against President Gorbachev in August 1991. Under Boris Yeltsin's presidency, he served seventeen months in prison for his involvement in the coup until he was pardoned by parliament in 1994. He owed his full rehabilitation to his former KGB subordinate Lieutenant Colonel Vladimir Putin, when the latter became president. As pointed out by the Moscow correspondent Masha Gessen, his presence among the 1,500 guests at Putin's inauguration reflected a regime change that Kryuchkov obviously welcomed wholeheartedly.

Our meeting in 2005 took place in the presence of his daughter in a spacious, tastefully furnished four-room apartment, which he had moved into after his rehabilitation by Putin. He had often been a guest of the president, whose policies he fully supported, he told me. After our conversation, he gave me two books of his memoirs, which he had published after Putin took office. I thought of the terrible days in the air-raid shelter of our house in Budapest after the massive attack by Russian tanks on 4 November 1956 and the shocking image of our destroyed apartment. And now, almost half a century later, this friendly conversation with a contemporary witness of evil about the behind-the-scenes secrets of the hated victors: what a contrast. It was difficult for the 81-year-old man to stand; he died two years after our interview.

Mikhail Gorbachev: an exceptional phenomenon

Chance played a major role in my encounters with two victims and two "desk perpetrators" during the transition from the Soviet system through the brief, failed democratic experiment under Boris Yeltsin to Vladimir Putin's dictatorship.

And I was lucky enough to twice meet Mikhail Gorbachev, the most unique and historically important personality since Joseph Stalin. We in the West admired him as the real destroyer of the Soviet system and the Eastern bloc, even though his goal until the end had been to keep both together. For most Russians, however, he was the politician who gambled away Stalin's legacy after six years in power (1985–1991). Consequently, he only received 0.5 per cent of the vote in the relatively free presidential elections in 1996. The enormous international response to his death on 30 August 2022, thirty years after his fall, reflected the enduring fascination with this extraordinary personality.

The fact that Gorbachev was remembered in his home country as a deeply contradictory figure was something I experienced in June 1992 in a small group at a meeting of the Bertelsmann Foundation's Eastern Europe Working Group in Moscow. On his way to our hotel, the ex-president possibly experienced the hatred of broad sections of the population at first hand. With the benevolent toleration of the police, several thousand demonstrators from the still communist-controlled trade unions had organised loud protests against Gorbachev in front of the office of the foundation he established with money from the Nobel Peace Prize on Leningradsky Prospekt. As he had been in Haifa shortly before to receive an Israeli peace prize, several demonstrators carried anti-Semitic or anti-Israel posters. Gorbachev had to leave the building through the back exit; he arrived late and was visibly agitated. At the beginning, I almost had the impression that he was on the verge of crying. His voice choking with tears, he began a short digression. He seemed like a broken man who couldn't come to terms with the fact of his sudden fall. He bitterly criticised the state of affairs in Russia and especially his hated successor, Boris Yeltsin.

Ten years later, he spoke more optimistically about the economic situation in Russia to an audience of five hundred people at a panel discussion I chaired in

Vienna. He assured me that he supported the "course of stabilisation" of President Vladimir Putin, who had been elected two years earlier. For him, Yeltsin remained the enemy who had destroyed democracy. He also later avoided taking a clear stance against Putin, never criticised his foreign policy course, and defended the annexation of Crimea in 2014.

Before his illness, his foundation, which supports socio-economic and political research, was financed not only by the lecture fees of between $20,000 and $50,000 he normally received, but also by his appearing in worldwide advertising for Pizza Hut and Louis Vuitton. Of course, these were never shown in Russia itself. His enemies claimed that he had sold out to the Americans, although his very efforts to finance the foundation were proof that Gorbachev was never corrupt.

Putin did not grant his predecessor a state funeral. Alexei Navalny, Putin's most dangerous opponent, who died in an Arctic prison at the age of 48 in February 2024, wrote from prison that he had been convinced that future generations would appreciate Gorbachev more than his contemporaries had done, as he never used his power to enrich himself and left his post voluntarily.

The encounters described here, as well as other experiences on trips abroad, should serve to explain my rejection of all forms of political hypocrisy, of pomposity dictated by profit, of false pathos in dealing with the cruel past of war, and of covering up the guilt of autocrats and dictators. The unusual fates that I describe expose the political hypocrisy that still flourishes today in dealing with Russia's contemporary history. They remind us of the violence used to silence opposition under the dictatorship of Vladimir Putin, of how the true masterminds of political murders are covered up, and how high-ranking desk criminals remain in power and are courted abroad.

2

THE SOVIET UNION

THE MARCH THROUGH DISILLUSIONMENT

Dead people change their political views effortlessly.

Stanisław Jerzy Lec

The great Czech poet-president Václav Havel once declared: "We live in a postmodern world in which everything is possible and almost nothing is certain."[1] These words, spoken in 1998, criticised the contradictory attitude of the West towards the states of Central and Eastern Europe that had become free. They still apply today and are almost prophetic in view of the emergence of autocratic regimes in Eastern Europe and the threat to liberal democracies posed by the war of aggression waged against Ukraine by a nationalist Russian dictatorship obsessed with imperial dreams.

Why have Western politicians and commentators been so often and for so long mistaken in their assessment of developments in Russia, and what are the presumed causes of the passivity of European Union bodies towards the authoritarian course set by the governments in Hungary and (between 2015 and 2023) in Poland?

When talking about interpretations and misinterpretations of Russian and Eastern European politics since the fall of communism between 1989 and 1991, one must not forget the naive claims, exaggerated expectations and disappointed hopes from the seventy-year history of the Soviet Union and communist regimes from China to Cuba. It is not only the enormous global propaganda campaigns of the communist parties or the activities of the numerous spies who worked for the Soviet Union or the Warsaw Pact states that are responsible for this.

Deluded admirers of Stalin

I would first like to look at the enduring impact of those intellectuals and journalists that the US sociologist Paul Hollander (1932–2019) called "political pilgrims" in his seminal work of the same name, which is subtitled "Western intellectuals in search of the good society".[2] In his book, first published in 1981 and later expanded in several new editions, Hollander uses the examples of Jean-Paul Sartre and Simone de Beauvoir, George Bernard Shaw and Edmund Wilson, Noam Chomsky and Susan Sontag, to analyse the reasons why they admired the communist dictatorships in the Soviet

Union, China and Cuba and rejected their own Western liberal societies. In a detailed supplement to the new edition following the collapse of the Eastern bloc, he also cites North Korea, Latin America, Cambodia and Vietnam as examples, and supplements the list of prominent intellectual pilgrims.

One of the most impressive quotes in the book is a sentence written by the British writer Graham Greene in a letter to the London *Times* in 1967: "If I had to choose between life in the Soviet Union and life in the United States, I would certainly choose the Soviet Union, just as I would rather live in Cuba than in the South American republics [...] or in North Vietnam than in South Vietnam." According to his US editor, Greene had a weakness for countries that seemed to challenge the West, especially the United States, and that he believed were victims of the West.[3]

Greene was not alone, of course. Hollander describes the praise of famous authors for living conditions in the Soviet Union with many bizarre details that seem almost unbelievable today in view of the horrors of the Stalin era. In a time of famine, show trials and mass terror, outstanding authors such as George Bernard Shaw, Lion Feuchtwanger and H. G. Wells praised Stalin and his regime out of naivety or calculation. The only but significant exception was André Gide, the French Nobel Prize winner for literature, who published a disappointed and highly critical report on his impressions after a two-month tour in 1936 under the title *Return from the USSR*. As a kind of counterpart, Lion Feuchtwanger wrote *Moscow 1937* a little later. In it, after a two-month stay, he praised the living conditions in the Soviet Union to the skies, defended the Moscow show trials as legitimate and, after Stalin had granted him a two-hour audience, celebrated him as a "great organiser, calculator and psychologist" and as a "type of Russian peasant and worker elevated to genius". Today, thanks to documentation published in 2017, which includes many letters, notes and secret files, we know that Feuchtwanger was neither naive nor a victim of Soviet propaganda, but rather used it against his better judgement out of his own interests.[4]

One of the first official conversations with Stalin was conducted in 1931 by the German writer Emil Ludwig, who was world-famous at the time for his biographies.[5] Throughout the three-hour interview, there were no questions or objections from Ludwig, even when Stalin made obvious false statements. In his book with short biographies of nine leading European personalities (published in 1934), Ludwig confessed: "I had expected a Grand Duke of the old regime—strict, brusque and unfriendly. Instead, I met for the first time a dictator to whom I would willingly entrust the education of my children. A lonely man, not influenced by money or pleasure or even ambition. Although he has enormous power at his disposal, he does not enjoy the possession of power, although he should feel a certain degree of satisfaction that he has triumphed over his opponents."[6] Feuchtwanger found Stalin to be the "simplest of all the rulers" he had met, "prepared to endure criticism and to respond to candour with candour".[7]

But it was not only intellectuals who were blinded by Stalin. The US ambassador to Moscow from 1936 to 1939, Joseph E. Davies, who later defended the Soviet show trials in his book *Mission to Moscow*, was repeatedly charmed by Stalin's modest personality: "His brown eyes are extraordinarily wise and gentle. A child would love to sit on his lap, and a dog would sneak up on him."[8] The socialist sociologist couple Beatrice and Sidney Webb (1858–1943 and 1859–1947 respectively) quoted Stalin, who was statistically responsible for more deaths than Hitler, affirmatively and ironically: "Man must be educated as carefully and attentively as a gardener grows his beloved fruit tree."[9] Ambassador Davies's book was translated into several languages, sold more than 700,000 copies, and was praised by most of the world's press as a definitive work. In 1943, a film with the same title was made under the direction of Michael Curtiz. During the Second World War, Davies was sent on a special mission to deliver a confidential letter from President Franklin D. Roosevelt to Stalin and subsequently served as a special advisor to the president and his successor, Harry S. Truman.

Among the journalists who, for whatever reason, misled the political and business elite in the United States for decades about the terrible conditions during the Stalin era, Walter Duranty, *New York Times* Moscow bureau chief from 1922 to 1936 and Pulitzer Prize winner in 1932, was one of the most important. He was praised by Stalin, who even granted him an interview in 1933, for his "truthful reportage".[10] When Stalin starved millions of Ukrainians to accelerate forced collectivisation in the Soviet Union, Duranty defended the dictator in the *New York Times* in March 1933 with the infamous sentence "You can't make an omelette without breaking eggs". Duranty's remarks later led to a debate about whether he had deliberately lied or merely parroted Stalinist propaganda. There were also repeated calls (which continue to this day) for him to be retrospectively stripped of his Pulitzer Prize.[11] Even if the Moscow correspondents of other Western newspapers contradicted him at the time, the mendacious reporting of the most respected US newspaper undoubtedly had great influence on the foreign policy of the Roosevelt administration.

Swimming trunks as an instrument of politics

Seemingly intimate meetings between autocrats and carefully selected foreign personalities from politics and the media run like a red thread through the history of Russia, Cuba, China and Vietnam as a tried and tested means of image cultivation. Two curious and grotesque stories about such meetings involved swimming trunks!

In the summer of 1963, a select group of writers, including Simone de Beauvoir and Jean-Paul Sartre, were flown on a special aeroplane from a conference in Leningrad via Moscow to Nikita Khrushchev's summer residence in Gagra on the Black Sea coast in Georgia. The German writer Hans Magnus Enzensberger describes the meeting and the Soviet party leader's fifty-minute-long, rather confused speech in his book *Tumult*. He notes with astonishment the lack of charisma of the man who, after all, had prevailed against powerful rivals and initiated the de-Stalinisation process: "His merits can best be defined in negative terms. He is quite free of the delusions of grandeur and persecution of his predecessors. His basic convictions are so simple that they do not programme his behaviour, but the other way round: behaviour interprets them from case to case. Within the limits of his commonplaces, he is uncertain and therefore teachable. He has no idea of his greatest political achievement. It lies in the demystification of power. A man without a secret at the head of the state: that is rare in the world; in Russia it is unheard of [...] You may yawn at this man's table, but you don't feel threatened."[12] Enzensberger is so relaxed that he even goes swimming in the Black Sea with Khrushchev in a pair of swimming trunks that are far too big for him. Visibly proud, he immediately reported to his publisher Siegfried Unseld that the general secretary had lent him his swimming trunks.[13] Three years later, he travelled the USSR from the far south to Siberia.

Almost forty years later, the former editor-in-chief of *Bild*, the largest circulation German daily, Kai Diekmann, also reported in his memoirs how Vladimir Putin, in office as president for just over a year, invited him to swim together after an interview at his private dacha in Sochi, stripped naked in front of the German visitors, and forced Diekmann to wear one of his tight swimming trunks. This is followed by his impressions in the course of further interviews during Putin's rise to an unchallenged position of power.[14]

In *Political Pilgrims*, Hollander describes how the carefully organised round trips in special trains or special compartments with accommodation in the best hotels, the encounters with alleged readers or critics, and the reliable and skilful interpreters contributed to the encapsulation and delusion of the intellectuals and artists visiting Russia.

Soviet-friendly experts

In the whitewashing of the Russian and Eastern European dictatorships of the twentieth century, so-called Eastern experts played an important role both in academic research and in the environment of foreign ministries and the media. Personalities from the academic elite and many experts went so far as to claim to be able to predict or even influence the decisions of local politicians based on their knowledge of the East. In what follows, we will cite memorable examples from politics, business and the media from recent times that show the urge to assert oneself and, in some cases, to justify a policy of hypocrisy.

It is instructive and useful to recall the opinion-forming effect of the experts of the time and their influence on political decisions. Looking back at commentaries on Soviet policy from a distance of up to half a century is an amusing but at the same time unsettling experience. The historian Walter Laqueur (1921–2018) was the author of one of the first comprehensive works on interpretations and misinterpretations of Soviet history.[15] In a review of his memoirs, *Best of Times, Worst of Times*, which he published at the age of 88, it was said that anyone following Laqueur through the twentieth century was embarking on a march through disillusionment. For there were not only romantically inclined authors or idealistic intellectuals, but also scientists and diplomats in Paris, London and New York who were prepared to enthusiastically support Stalin and the Soviet Union during the period of mass terror in the 1930s and even more so after the Allied victory over Hitler's Germany.

After a visit to the Soviet Union in the mid-1930s, for example, the British political scientist and economist Harold Laski (1893–1950) saw "not much difference between the general character of a trial in Russia and in our country", and he praised the notorious chief prosecutor of the Moscow trials, Andrei Vyshinsky, after an interview as "an ideal Minister of Justice for Great Britain".[16]

The American ambassador Joseph E. Davies, a multi-millionaire and successful lawyer, had no doubts about the guilt of the defendants in the Moscow show trials. "It then came to light that a small number of leading personalities were infected by the poison of the conspiracy spirit and were actually working with the organisations of the German and Japanese secret services. Frankly, one cannot blame those in power for reacting as they did if they believed what is now being revealed in this trial."[17] In his book *Mission to Moscow*, he included a reference to a lecture he gave to a university club three years later: "It was exactly three days after Hitler's invasion of Russia. Someone in the audience asked: 'And what about the fifth column in Russia?' Without hesitation, I replied: 'No such thing! All shot.'"[18]

Ambassador Davies was by no means alone. Professor Bernard Pares, the leading British expert on Russian and Soviet affairs, had a similar view of the Moscow show trials and purges. "We need not doubt the trials, no matter how the evidence may originally have been obtained. In any case, the extensive verbatim interrogation protocols were impressive."[19] Laqueur's dry comment on this was: "The longer the indictment, the greater its truthfulness. So that was the result of fifty years of studying Russian history, the Russian people, their country, their language ..."[20]

This kind of pro-Soviet and pro-Russian bias was significantly reinforced by films and novels in the United States and Great Britain during the great alliance of the Second World War and was only largely, but by no means universally, demythologised in the decades of the Cold War. One of the most respected and at the same time most controversial British historians, Edward Hallett Carr (1892–1982), author of a fourteen-volume history of the Soviet Union between 1917 and 1929, sometime diplomat and editorial writer for the London *Times*, was fascinated by power and rulers, by Hitler and Stalin, and refused to make moral judgements. Carr's belief that there were no universal standards of morality, as events in each country could only be judged in their particular context, was sharply criticised by many historians and political scientists and was seen as a combination of professional expertise on the one hand and moral indifference on the other.

Learning from mistakes?

As we have seen, Walter Laqueur analysed interpretations and misinterpretations of Soviet history from 1917 to the 1980s.[21] This could be extended by drawing on further examples from the time of Mikhail Gorbachev and Boris Yeltsin. An extensive library could in fact be compiled from the reports, stories and autobiographies of the perpetrators, victims and followers, often characterised by blind love and blind hatred. I will come back to the perfected sham plausibility and cynical hypocrisy of the Putin regime in adopting the props from the arsenal of Great Russian nationalism.

This summary from the early days of the Soviet system about unsuspecting idealists and seduced experts in need of reassurance may seem like a superfluous collection of quotations in view of the collapse of the Soviet system and its ideological foundations. But, as the German poet and philosopher Friedrich Schlegel (1772–1829) wrote, historians are backward-looking prophets. Like the immediate aftermath of the Russian Revolution, the *annus mirabilis* of 1989–1990 was characterised by illusory expectations and unfulfilled hopes. Examining historical lessons can serve as a warning against repeating the mistakes and political failures that have arisen from them.

Just as the admonishers of Hitler's Germany in London and Washington in the late 1930s remained lonely criers in the wilderness, most Western politicians could not afford to get too far ahead of public opinion in their warnings of a threat to European peace from the revanchist Putin regime, which had been looming since 2007, had been clear since the annexation of Crimea in 2014 and had been imminent since 2020.

The economic sector represents a chapter on its own. After Lenin proclaimed a new economic policy (NEP) in 1921 with a free market and profit-oriented thinking in order to avoid total collapse as a result of war communism during the civil war, the positive reaction of previously ostracised businessmen and Western politicians was not long in coming. Lenin was even credited with the following sentence, variously expressed: "The capitalists will sell us the rope with which we hang them." There is actually no evidence that Lenin ever said that.

The actual interest of Western investors is a different matter. It is often forgotten that long before Chancellor Willy Brandt's Ostpolitik towards communist East Germany, characterised by the popular slogan "change through trade", the liberal British prime minister David Lloyd George expressed a similar idea, albeit exaggerated in contemporary jargon, in a parliamentary speech on 12 February 1922: "In my opinion, trade will put an end to Bolshevism more surely than any other method of cruelty, violence and primitiveness. I believe we can save Russia through trade."[22]

After 1989–1990, following the collapse of the communist systems and thus of the Russian colonial empire, most Western politicians and political and economic observers believed just as emphatically that the globalisation of the economy would pave the way for the triumphal march of democracy from Budapest to Moscow. In contrast, Vladimir Putin, lieutenant colonel in the Soviet secret service KGB, like most senior Soviet officials, officers and secret service agents, regarded the collapse of the Soviet Union as "the greatest geopolitical catastrophe of the twentieth century".[23] The many varieties of hypocrisy served as a trivialising bridge between the two extremes, the prophets of globalisation and liberal democracy on the one hand and the nationalist autocrats obsessed with revanchism on the other. And so the march through disillusionment that began in 1917 reached a new climax with the start of Russia's war of aggression against Ukraine on 24 February 2022.

3

GERMANY'S BLIND RUSSIA POLICY

It's hard to tell who is voluntarily swimming with the current.

Stanisław Jerzy Lec

How was it possible that German politicians, especially leading Social Democrats, but also the long-term chancellor Angela Merkel, have failed to recognise, played down and in some cases denied the danger of Russian aggression despite many warning signs since 2007, and particularly since the annexation of Crimea in 2014? Why were the reports and warnings from Poland and the Baltic states, by Russian opposition figures and human rights activists, by Western journalists and contemporary historians, ignored? What political and economic interests, what personal and business connections, led to the European Union's strongest economic power becoming dependent on Putin's Russia in terms of energy policy? How did German politics and business come to rely on

Vladimir Putin, even though he had already pursued an aggressive foreign policy and brutally suppressed the opposition years before his invasion of Ukraine?

It is a stroke of luck for modern German history and for future historians that the first authentic answer to these thorny questions comes from a man who played a decisive role in shaping German history in the twentieth century, both from below and from above. It is Joachim Gauck, the eleventh (and first non-party) federal president of the Federal Republic of Germany from 2012 to 2017, who, together with his co-author Helga Hirsch, has written a work entitled *Erschütterungen* (Shocks)—an almost passionate, unsparing analysis of the "blindness to reality" of German politics.[1]

Joachim Gauck, born in 1940, can look back on three different phases in his life. Until 1989, he worked as an Evangelical Lutheran pastor in Rostock and played an important role in the resistance of the Church against the communist regime in East Germany (GDR). I met Joachim Gauck at an international conference organised by Melvin Lasky, editor-in-chief of *Encounter* magazine, in Berlin in autumn 1992. Gauck was then (from 1990 to 2000) federal commissioner for the records of the State Security Service of the GDR. He described in a lecture the structure and work of this invisible secret police network with 90,000 full-time employees and, as late as 1989, around 170,000 so-called informal collaborators, that is, agents and informers. As I wanted to find out what was available about me in the Stasi archives, I asked Gauck for access to my files during a personal conversation after his lecture. A subsequent exchange of letters revealed that there were some "documents of contemporary historical interest" about me. In the summer of 1993, I was then able to obtain explosive documents from the Stasi archive involving the correspondence (from 1965!) between the Hungarian and East German interior ministers as a prelude to a subsequent, almost Eastern bloc-wide visa ban against me. This astonishing evidence laid the tracks to later, much richer finds in the secret service archives of Hungary and Czechoslovakia. All of this then found a fitting place in my autobiography.[2]

Joachim Gauck's exemplary stance

In retrospect, Federal President Gauck's unambiguous stance following the Russian annexation of Crimea and the Kremlin's open support for the pro-Russian separatists in eastern Ukraine is still exemplary today, even internationally. It lends his time in office a special significance. In stark contrast to the Russia policy of his successor, Frank-Walter Steinmeier, Gauck didn't mince his words in his first term as federal president, even as early as 2014.[3]

On 1 September 2014, on the occasion of a speech given in Gdańsk at the invitation of the Polish president on the 75th anniversary of the outbreak of the Second World War, he said: "Because we uphold the law, because we strengthen it and do not tolerate it being replaced by the law of the strongest, we oppose those who break international law, annex foreign territory and support militarily secession in foreign countries." He added: "History teaches us that territorial concessions often only increase the appetite of aggressors."[4]

The condemnation of Russia's aggressive policy was criticised by left-wing and left-liberal journalists and historians as a "presidential blunder of the first order", as "a careless escalation of words".[5] At the time, well-known public figures—from feminist Alice Schwarzer to former German chancellor Helmut Schmidt and the architect of Germany's Ostpolitik, Egon Bahr—played down the annexation of Crimea and even expressed understanding for Putin. Joachim Gauck, on the other hand, went to Kiev as German president on 22 February 2015 to take part in a "March of Dignity" of 10,000 people, together with the presidents of Poland, Lithuania and Ukraine. They commemorated the more than 100 victims killed in the pro-European demonstrations on Maidan, the central square of the Ukrainian capital, the year before and the 5,000 dead fighters against the pro-Russian separatists in the Donbas.

Even at the time of the criticism of Gauck's Gdańsk speech, the former Polish foreign minister Władysław Bartoszewski, the later Nobel Prize winner for literature

Olga Tokarczuk and other Polish intellectuals warned of the consequences of an appeasement policy towards Putin: "Anyone who does not shout 'No pasarán' [They shall not pass] at Putin today is making a mockery of the European Union and its values and consenting to the world order being overturned. Yesterday Gdańsk, today Donetsk [...] We must not allow Europe to live with an open, bleeding wound for many years to come."[6]

Gauck, who describes himself as a "left-wing, liberal conservative" and "enlightened patriot", emphasises in retrospect that the turning point came in 2014 at the latest: "The Poles saw it, many politicians and intellectuals in Germany and Europe did not want to see it." Based on this conclusion, Gauck searches for the roots of the "mistakes of an Ostpolitik that unwaveringly wanted to believe that all of humanity, with its longing for peace, would strive for the goal of a generally accepted peace that would transcend all systemic differences [...] and that Germany could play a mediating role between 'the West' and Russia".[7]

The Germans' false image of Russia

When the question is asked about the roots of the special concern on the part of Germany towards Russia, three main reasons are generally cited. Hitler's Germany incurred an immeasurable debt by committing crimes against the peoples of the Soviet Union during the

Second World War, and the Germans therefore bear a special responsibility for European peace. Furthermore, the Soviet Union played an outstanding role in the liberation of Germany from Hitler's regime. And, finally, the Germans owe the unification of Germany to Mikhail Gorbachev and the Soviet government in view of the Soviet withdrawal of troops from East Germany.

This mixture of gratitude and guilt has shaped German attitudes towards Russia in recent decades. The fact that East Germany and Eastern Europe were at the mercy of Soviet tyranny for almost half a century did nothing to change this. It is a bizarre twist in present-day history that Vladimir Putin was able to exploit for two decades the deeply felt gratitude towards his peaceful predecessor Gorbachev as political capital for his aggressive goals.

The widespread ignorance about Ukraine, which is after all the second-largest country in Europe in terms of area with 44 million inhabitants, prepared the ground for the deliberate political hypocrisy of Russian propaganda. As a rule, and not only in German-speaking countries, the figure of 27 million Soviet victims in the Second World War was almost exclusively identified with the "Russians". From the very beginning, however, Soviet historiography concealed the Holocaust. The millions of murdered Jews were added to the mass of "victims of fascism". This type of counting also drew in the 8 million war victims in Ukraine, more than 5 million of whom were civilians, including 1.5 million Jews.

The distorted image of Russia in Germany also involved arrogance towards the Poles, Lithuanians, Latvians, Estonians and Ukrainians, which was partly the result of ignorance. For many years, these nations with their traumatic experiences during the Soviet era were regarded as troublemakers who harboured exaggerated anti-Russian resentment. In the meantime, events have confirmed that their assessment of Putin's policies was much more realistic than the lenient attitude of Germany, Austria and other EU states, which was driven solely by economic interests.

The special relationship between Berlin and Moscow was not only linked to the network around the ex-chancellor and friend of Putin Gerhard Schröder. None of the top Western politicians met Putin as often as Angela Merkel during her sixteen years as German chancellor. No other EU member state regularly sent as many delegations to Russia for business talks as the Federal Republic of Germany.

The strangely positive image of Russia on both the right and the left in Germany should not be overlooked. Russia's appeal to the left derives from its traditional condemnation of the United States as a hypocritical imperialist world power whose policy is shaped not by officially proclaimed values, but by geostrategic and economic interests. The right-wing populists and national conservatives, on the other hand, despise the allegedly decadent culture of America, which is far too tolerant of lesbians and gays. They crave a strongman at the apex of the state. The Victory Day reception at the Russian embassy in Berlin in May 2023 provided a highly symbolic image. Former Social Democratic chancellor Gerhard Schröder was joined there by the leader of the far-right AfD party, Tino Chrupalla, who wore a tie in the colours of the Russian flag, and by Chrupalla's predecessor, Alexander Gauland. The last general secretary of the Communist Party ruling in East Germany, Egon Krenz, was also present.[8]

Political statements reflect the shared sympathy of the extreme right and left for Russia. If he had to choose between the "globalist West" and the "traditional East", said Björn Höcke from the radical right wing of the AfD, he would choose the East.[9] Sahra Wagenknecht, who has since founded a new left-wing populist party, has repeatedly spoken out in favour of a halt to arms deliveries to Ukraine and unconditional negotiations with the Kremlin.[10]

The failure of Germany's Russia policy

Let us turn back to the forgotten, suppressed and therefore still highly revealing failure of Western, especially German, policy towards Russia between 2014 (annexation of Crimea) and 2022 (invasion of Ukraine). Joachim Gauck is the first top German politician to address Angela Merkel's responsibility for the course she took at the time, and refute her attempts to justify it. She repeatedly claimed that the Minsk Agreement of September 2014, which attempted to achieve a ceasefire in eastern Ukraine with Germany, among others, was an effort to "give Ukraine time". And Ukraine also used this "valuable time" to "become stronger".[11]

In his book, Gauck openly states that the German government has let Ukraine down on several occasions.[12] With the Baltic Sea pipelines for Russian gas, which bypass Ukraine as a transit country, the German government made Ukraine more susceptible to blackmail. Furthermore, Germany even tried to stop the United States from supplying weapons to Ukraine in 2015. According to Gauck, German diplomacy in Poland and the Baltic states was already seen at the time as "naive and submissive". The sanctions were half-hearted and had no real effect. It was only two days before the Russian attack on Ukraine that the Nord Stream 2 pipeline project, which had been criticised internationally from all sides, was halted.

In retrospect, Angela Merkel can be asked the same questions as those raised by Gauck: "Why, despite this clarity [about Putin's plans], she continued to stick solely to the 'soft' methods in dealing with Putin, why, despite his lies, she trusted that it was ultimately a predictable relationship, why she defended Nord Stream 2 until the end of her term of office and emphasised that Russia had always been a stable supplier of energy: all this is difficult to decipher and may never be fully clarified."[13]

What is certain is that all German governments have underestimated Putin and, as Gauck emphasises, "thereby weakened Germany politically, economically, militarily and mentally and made it partially dependent".[14] Gauck spares no one, and he recalls the broad understanding in German politics and society for the aggressor Putin with shockingly naive quotes from the appeal signed by sixty well-known personalities in December 2014, "War in Europe again? Not in our name!"

Propagandistic help for Putin

I was most taken aback by Helmut Schmidt's statements at the time. The respected former Social Democratic chancellor (1974–1982) found Putin's actions "quite understandable" and considered sanctions to be "stupid stuff".[15] In an interview with *Bild*, the popular daily, Schmidt even denied the existence of a Ukrainian nation.[16] As he died shortly afterwards, he was no longer able to read the great books by Serhii Plokhy, the Ukrainian Harvard historian, on the history of Ukraine and Russia's war of aggression. These describe the nation-building of the Ukrainians and the consequences of Russian aggression.[17]

Quite apart from current events, we must never forget the referendum held in Ukraine on 1 December 1991. At that time, with a turnout of 84 per cent, over 90 per cent of the voters were already in favour of

Ukrainian independence, 92.88 per cent in Kiev, 83 per cent in Donbas and 54 per cent in Crimea. The Russian invasion has given a huge boost to the process of strengthening the Ukrainian nation. The drones, the missiles, the bombs from Russia make no difference to the victims, whether their mother tongue is originally Russian or Ukrainian. When I once listened to President Volodymyr Zelensky's impassioned speech in Ukrainian on the night after the invasion and recalled that he is of Jewish origin and his mother tongue is Russian, I remembered the famous lecture by the French historian Ernest Renan on the nation: "In a person there is something that is superior to language: the will [...] A nation is therefore a great community of solidarity, sustained by the feeling of the sacrifices one has made and the sacrifices one is still willing to make [...] The existence of a nation is—allow me this image—a daily plebiscite."[18]

Even if hardly any serious person in the West today would doubt the existence of the fighting Ukrainian community of will, it remains questionable, and not only for Joachim Gauck, whether a majority of Germans would be prepared to defend liberal democracy resolutely. Even after the invasion of Ukraine on 24 February 2022, concerns about the danger of a world war and nuclear war were repeatedly expressed in appeals, manifestos and statements. The 96-year-old philosopher Jürgen Habermas declared a few weeks after the start of the Russian war of aggression, "in view of the risk of a world conflagration that must be avoided at all costs": "Now that the West has decided not to intervene in this conflict as a warring party, there is a risk threshold that rules out unrestrained involvement in arming Ukraine." The West would have to "carefully weigh up with every further step of military support whether it is crossing the indeterminate line of formal entry into the war, which depends on Putin's power of definition."[19]

Ten months later, Habermas emphasised in a comprehensive but essentially inconclusive new "plea for negotiations" that "a face-saving compromise could be found for both sides".[20] There are "no promising conditions for negotiations, but no hopeless ones either". However, he himself lists the fait accompli (the annexation of the eastern provinces) "which makes the start of promising negotiations almost impossible". He is concerned that we could end up facing the hopeless choice of "either actively intervening in the war or, in order to avoid triggering the first world war between nuclear-armed powers, abandoning Ukraine to its fate".

The response in the media was unfavourable because, according to the argument, Habermas was arguing for negotiations without saying when, about what and with whom one could negotiate. The political scientist Herfried Münkler criticised the tactical fallacy behind Habermas's appeal. Negotiations are "not the alternative to fighting", according to Münkler, but they have been taking place since the outbreak of war. That there was no negotiation in the background was a "fiction".[21]

However, in the tradition of German pacifism ("Never again war") as the founding ethos of the Federal Republic of Germany, this fiction attracted hundreds of thousands of people. They signed in spring 2023 the misleading "Manifesto for Peace" by Alice Schwarzer and Sahra Wagenknecht, which put attackers and defenders on the same level.[22] Much has been discussed and argued about the "excited self-talk" that has been going on in Germany since 24 February 2022: "It is primarily about the question of how it can give up its military restraint and still be one of the good guys, and why it should send weapons to the very region where the SS and Wehrmacht once murdered. It is in the nature of things and the digital public sphere that cleverer, stupider and more stupid contributions emerge in this self-talk," Sonja Zekri noted in the *Süddeutsche Zeitung*. She described it as an "intolerable" "German claim" that Wagenknecht, Schwarzer, Precht and Welzer assert that they know better what is good for Ukrainians than their own government in Kiev.[23]

There were even harsher comments. Gerhart Baum, the long-standing liberal interior minister in the social-liberal coalition led by Helmut Schmidt, described the illusion that peace should come at the expense of freedom as "the German disease": "It is the scepticism of quite a few Germans to defend freedom with weapons if necessary. This is incomprehensible—after all, we ourselves were liberated from Nazi barbarism with weapons! Proof of this is the widespread dissociation from NATO [...] A longing for peace without regard for the assertion of freedom leads to renewed aggression."[24]

Regardless of the fact that this very German debate, which is inextricably linked to the country's own history, is by no means only engaged in by representatives of the extremes, it must be said that the "Manifesto for Peace", including the TV appearances of the friends of peace, served as a valuable propaganda aid for the aggressor, Vladimir Putin.

Hypocrisy plays a special role in the reactions in Germany to Russia's aggression. The fear among Germans of a military escalation to the point of a nuclear strike is an important part of Putin's strategy. This is why Joachim Gauck's arguments against "self-deterrence", the fear of a decisive reaction, must be emphasised: "From the perspective of the invaded victim, the demand for an immediate ceasefire looks like this: Because politicians and intellectuals in the West cannot stand the horror of war, they, the invaded, should be obliged to give up their defence." Gauck draws the correct conclusion: "Anyone who *now* advocates a ceasefire in a partially occupied Ukraine is intentionally or unintentionally favouring Putin's side [...] As long as Putin does not accept an independent Ukrainian state, there will be no peace."[25] Gauck repeatedly calls on the West to be honest. In order to make possible a victory for Ukraine, arms deliveries must be massively increased in terms of quantity and quality.[26]

Although Angela Merkel's governments were also responsible for the failed Russia policy, the former chancellor Gerhard Schröder (1998–2005) and his comrades bear the main responsibility for the political and economic consequences of their Putin-friendly course.

4

FROM WILLY BRANDT TO GERHARD SCHRÖDER

THE SPLENDOUR AND MISERY OF SPD POLICY TOWARDS THE EAST

You can recognise by the backbone which era a person belongs to.

Stanisław Jerzy Lec

Is it true that the mixture of political naivety towards Putin's system and the resulting dependence on Russian gas has been the biggest mistake in German foreign policy since the founding of the German Federal Republic? And did the pro-Russian network around former chancellor Gerhard Schröder play a key role in this? These statements by Reinhard Bingener and Markus Wehner, the authors of the investigative book *Die Moskau-Connection: Das Schröder-Netzwerk und Deutschlands Weg in die Abhängigkeit* [The Moscow Connection: The Schröder Network and Germany's

Road to Dependence], are backed up with a wealth of facts and evidence.[1]

Willy Brandt's pioneering Ostpolitik

Even if the course was set between 1998 and 2021, the roots of the momentous mistakes committed by the German Social Democrats in their policy towards Russia cannot be understood without glancing at the Ostpolitik, which is inextricably linked with the name of Willy Brandt. This policy of détente advocated by Willy Brandt as federal chancellor (1969–1974) and his closest advisor, Egon Bahr, with the motto of "change through rapprochement", has become the myth of Social Democratic foreign policy. It has undoubtedly made a decisive contribution to overcoming the East–West confrontation of the Cold War.

I owe it to my personal closeness to former Austrian chancellor Bruno Kreisky (1970–1983) that I managed to meet Willy Brandt several times over the decades, both in private and in television discussion. Kreisky was active in the socialist movement and emigrated to Sweden shortly after the Anschluss in 1938 to avoid arrest. It was there that he met Willy Brandt, who had fled earlier from Germany via Norway to Sweden in 1940. The two political refugees, who were almost of the same age, became close friends in Stockholm. Working on my biography of Kreisky in 1971, I was able to have a long conversation with Brandt, then German chancellor, about his memories of the years of their cooperation in Sweden. An international discussion group led by Willy Brandt as secretary, the so-called Little Stockholm International, was important in this context. Kreisky and Brandt met almost every week at that time. In contrast to many German and Austrian social democrats, Kreisky was never in favour of a so-called pan-German revolution, but was always a man with a pronounced sense of Austrian identity. In personal terms, Kreisky had also changed less than most of the others Brandt knew from emigration, Brandt told me, and he added: "Even then, he was calm, Austrian, tolerant, patient, open to discussion—and tireless."[2]

I should actually have met Willy Brandt eight years earlier, during his time as mayor of Berlin. In November 1963, I was granted a journalist's visa as a *Financial Times* correspondent for an eight-day reporting trip to the GDR. During my stay, I also made an unusual detour to West Berlin. Kreisky, then Austrian foreign minister, had written to Willy Brandt and asked him to receive me for an interview. However, he was travelling in Asia and instead I was invited by his press spokesman, Egon Bahr, to a private meeting in his home. Although I was staying in the GDR government's guest house near the Wall (not as a guest, but at a horrendous price), and although the connection should have been particularly quick from here, it took twelve hours before I could be informed of the time and place of the meeting with Bahr. The GDR authorities spent a whole day considering whether to allow this "unusual" (as my official escort put it) detour. Today, it is hard to imagine such a procedure. The stimulating conversation with Egon Bahr, the most important mastermind of German Ostpolitik, made a strong impression on me even then. We agreed on the offensive orientation of the policy of détente. Six years later, I met him again at a Bilderberg conference in Denmark. As head of the political planning staff of the Foreign Ministry headed then by Willy Brandt, Bahr outlined, also in a confidential conversation with me, some of the ideas that would soon shape Germany's Ostpolitik.

In view of his background, his personal magnetism and his political courage, Willy Brandt became an icon of the Social Democratic Party (SPD). The very first conversation about his memories of Kreisky gave me the opportunity to become acquainted with the modesty, friendliness and openness of this exceptional personality. Over the years, there were repeated meetings in small circles, at various conferences and also during discussions broadcast by Austrian television. Both as federal chancellor and after his resignation, he always endeavoured to provide substantive answers to sensitive questions beyond the politics of the day and to emphasise social democratic perspectives.

The Ostpolitik of the social-liberal coalition government led by Chancellor Willy Brandt from 1969 onwards was based on the assumption that the existence of two states in Germany had to be recognised if this division was to be overcome in the long term. Renouncing the use of force, respecting the inviolability of borders in Europe, reducing tensions, and securing peace, good neighbourly relations and cooperation between the two blocs were the guiding principles of this so-called new Ostpolitik. The agreement that Egon Bahr negotiated for the Federal Republic of Germany with the Soviet Union in fifty hours of talks between January and May 1970 was of decisive importance. This Moscow Treaty, the core of which was the recognition of the Oder–Neisse border, paved the way for further treaties with Poland, the GDR and Czechoslovakia as well as for the Four-Power Agreement on Berlin in 1971.

By recognising the Oder–Neisse line as Poland's western border, the Federal Republic accepted the permanent loss of the former German eastern territories as a result of the Second World War, which Hitler's Germany had started and lost. With his prostration in front of the ghetto memorial in Warsaw in 1970, which caused a worldwide sensation, Brandt also acknowledged the guilt and responsibility of the Germans for the crimes committed by the Nazi regime. On behalf of his country, the chancellor silently asked for forgiveness.

Internationally, the Federal Republic of Germany gained through its new Ostpolitik the reputation of a universally respected partner committed to peace. This policy was not a German solo effort, but was firmly anchored in the Western alliance. It made a significant contribution to reducing tensions between the blocs and to minimising the risk of a military conflict. This was one of the reasons why Willy Brandt was awarded the Nobel Peace Prize in 1971.

The Helsinki Final Act of 1975 was the high point of Ostpolitik and, at the same time, of the European policy of détente, supported by the United States as the superpower protecting the free world. For the Soviet Union, it was about providing security and recognition of its European satellite empire. The West, on the other hand, hoped that the human rights obligations in the Helsinki Final Act would lead to the opening of the Eastern bloc states.

The wrong turn of SPD policy towards the East

As a commentator and reporter, I directly witnessed and described in detail the emergence of the trade union movement Solidarność (Solidarity) in Poland and the civil rights movement Charter 77 in Czechoslovakia in the 1970s and 1980s.[3] It was only in retrospect that I realised how a success story can lead to a historical aberration. This probably applies first and foremost to German social democracy, but there were also traces of this in Austria.

The hypocrisy in this second phase of SPD policy towards the East has been repeatedly addressed by the respected German historian (and also member of the SPD for sixty years) Heinrich August Winkler. He maintained that the leading Social Democrats felt no sympathy for the civil rights groups in the Eastern bloc countries. The SPD's relationship with them remained "characterised by cool distance, even mistrust". When Egon Bahr, then a member of the SPD's executive committee, was asked in autumn 1981 whether the Soviet Union had the right to intervene militarily in Poland if this country questioned its membership of the Warsaw Pact, his answer was "Of course". At the end of 1981, SPD chancellor Helmut Schmidt was of the opinion that the imposition of martial law in Poland on 13 December "was now necessary". During a visit to Poland in 1985, Willy Brandt avoided meeting Lech Wałesa, then leader of the Solidarność trade union.[4]

Winkler also points out that the oldest German party became a victim of its successes. In the 1980s, the realisation that military strength had been the necessary basis of the Western détente policy was forgotten. The collective memory in the SPD is characterised by the peace movement: "What is usually suppressed today is the price that the SPD demanded of the civil rights movements of the Eastern bloc in the second phase of Ostpolitik, which would probably not have existed at all without the first phase: for the sake of the stability of the East–West relationship, they were to resign themselves to their fate and continue to live in bondage."[5]

The policy of appeasement, always garnished with hypocrisy, marked the attitude towards the protest movements in the GDR until the very end. The SPD wanted nothing to do with reunification until immediately before the fall of the Wall. There are a wealth of statements about German reunification that seem bizarre today. Peter Glotz, the SPD's secretary general, called it (three weeks before the fall of the Wall) "opportunistic and repugnant". Gerhard Schröder labelled it "reactionary and highly dangerous". Egon Bahr spoke about its "political pollution".[6]

It is true that Willy Brandt also called reunification a "life lie" in 1984, but with his sense of the historical moment, he put his party on course for unity in 1989. After the fall of the Berlin Wall in 1990, Brandt admitted that the biggest miscalculation of his Ostpolitik had been not to trust the civil societies in the Eastern bloc to overthrow the regime. In contrast to Brandt, Egon Bahr remained close to Moscow until the end of his life. Even after the occupation of Crimea in 2014, he maintained his equidistance from Moscow and Washington.

Markus Meckel, the last foreign minister of the East German communist state, was the first prominent Social Democrat to openly and sharply criticise Egon Bahr's foreign policy line at an SPD event in Berlin at the end of October 2022. "In Brandt's name, Bahr pursued a fixation on Moscow that Brandt himself would never have gone along with. Meckel himself had always recommended that newly elected SPD chairmen visit Warsaw as the first capital in Eastern Europe, but Bahr, the icon, always placed them 'on Moscow's lap' first. With his critical stance on NATO and the US, Bahr had driven the SPD into the uncritical closeness to Russia for which they are paying so bitterly today."[7]

However, this critical statement, which was received with great grumbling by the audience, remained an exception. Egon Bahr continues to enjoy an almost "cult-like veneration" in parts of German social democracy, and a "demythicisation" is overdue. This was stated by Heinrich August Winkler in an analysis of the merits and misjudgements of the "left-wing nationalist" on the sixtieth anniversary of Bahr's speech on the slogan "change through rapprochement".[8]

Egon Bahr exerted a great influence on the SPD leadership after Brandt's death in 1992. For example, Matthias Platzeck, the former SPD chairman and prime minister of the state of Brandenburg, who expressed unlimited sympathy for Russia until the Ukraine war, called Egon Bahr his old master, whose most important guiding principle had been that there could only be lasting security with Russia. In July 2025 German media revealed that Platzek, Chairman of the German-Russian Forum from 2014 until February 2022, the invasion of the Ukraine undertook "at least nine secret trips to Moscow and Baku". Sometimes accompanied by other influential personalities, he had conducted talks with

Russian officials. He has been sharply criticised by Social Democratic politicians and historians.[9]

However, blindness towards Putin's Russia by no means only affects Platzeck or the network of Gerhard Schröder, who as chancellor and Putin's lobbyist set the most important course. For example, the former education minister in the first Brandt government and long-time mayor of Hamburg, Klaus von Dohnanyi, published a book called *Nationale Interessen* [National Interests][10] in early 2022, just a few weeks before the Russian invasion of Ukraine, which Joachim Gauck sharply condemned. In his book Dohnanyi accused "the allegedly aggressive, power-obsessed, anti-Russian America of having developed a 'Russia-phobia' and of demonising Putin", and he clung to the image of a threatened Russia. Dohnanyi even went so far as to express understanding for the creation of a "secure glacis", that is, a Russian imperial sphere of influence. Gauck, who had had to live in such a "safe glacis", namely under the East German communist regime for four decades, found this pro-Russian attitude of the Social Democrat particularly "bitter and outrageous".[11]

It was not until eight months after the Russian invasion that SPD chairman Lars Klingbeil acknowledged in a speech four mistakes in his party's dealings with Russia. Firstly, the Social Democrats had clung to an image of Russia that was characterised by the past but no longer reflected the present. Secondly, it had failed to recognise that the principle of change through rapprochement had not worked; the corresponding assumptions of Russia policy had not been checked for their reality and critically reflected upon. Thirdly, Germany had made itself dependent on Russia with its energy policy. Fourthly and finally, the interests of Eastern and Central European partners had not been sufficiently taken into account.[12] Klingbeil, who himself was quite active in promoting contacts with Russia, remained silent about why a different policy was not pursued, as did other top functionaries who were compromised by their proximity to the Kremlin. It is indicative of the mood barometer of the SPD's friendliness towards Russia that numerous prominent Social Democrats signed an appeal for peace in the spring of 2023 and called for a ceasefire in Ukraine "in continuation of the earlier policy of détente".[13]

Gerhard Schröder, "Putin's errand boy"

Former chancellor Gerhard Schröder and his extensive network are primarily responsible for the fateful blunders of the SPD's Ostpolitik over the past twenty-five years. It is likely that novels and plays will be written about the transformation of an SPD German chancellor into "Putin's best man in Germany".[14] In their aforementioned book *Die Moskau-Connection* by Reinhard Bingener and Markus Wehner about Germany's path to dependence on Russia, the reader will find the most thorough exploration and description to date of the unprecedentedly close personal, financial and political relations between Gerhard Schröder and Vladimir Putin. The authors conclude by raising the question why Schröder did not take a different path after his chancellorship. "Out of defiance, greed and stubbornness? His behaviour still remains a mystery."[15]

And Putin? Regardless of Schröder's personal motives, the standard answer from the dictionary of political hypocrisy is: "He deceived us all!" However, it should not be forgotten that Putin is a product of the KGB, the secret service. Its methods are known to include deception, lies and manipulation in its espionage abroad as well as intimidation, blackmail and the use of violence in its repression at home, including even the murder of "traitors" wherever they are. However, the romance between Putin and Schröder, as well as the "rapprochement through integration" proclaimed by Frank-Walter Steinmeier as foreign minister, has not been disturbed at all by the barbaric Chechen war, the eradication of independent media, and the murder of regime critics, from Anna Politkovskaya (2006) to Boris Nemtsov (2015).

A few figures show the development of the uniquely close personal relationship between Schröder and Putin. In the first two years after Putin took office, the two met eleven times, and Schröder avoided any public criticism of the human rights situation in Russia. Putin was the only foreign head of state to attend Schröder's sixtieth birthday celebrations in Hannover: German–Russian relations had "reached a depth that has never been seen before", said Schröder. In the last year of his chancellorship, 2005, Schröder met with Putin eight times, and around forty times altogether during his chancellorship.[16]

Shortly after being voted out of office as chancellor, Schröder took the public step, unprecedented in the history of the Federal Republic of Germany, from whitewashing Putin as a "flawless democrat "[17] to becoming the world's best-known lobbyist for Russia. He was appointed chairman of the shareholders' committee of the Nord Stream gas pipeline, in which the Russian state-owned company Gazprom holds a majority stake, with a salary of 250,000 euros, as well as chairman of the board of directors of the Nord Stream 2 gas pipeline, whose commissioning was stopped by Federal Chancellor Olaf Scholz following the Russian invasion of Ukraine. Despite the annexation of Crimea, Schröder also became a member of the supervisory board of the Russian energy company Rosneft, earning around 600,000 euros a year. He has since resigned from this position. He is said to have earned more than a million a year from his various posts. His total assets are now estimated at 20 million euros.[18]

The most important people to set the course for the policy of energy dependence on Russia were mostly former ministers from Gerhard Schröder's cabinet or successors at the top of the party or in the office of head of government of Lower Saxony. The network whose members directly or indirectly helped shape Angela Merkel's government policy emerged in the state capital of Hannover. There is no doubt that Frank-Walter Steinmeier played a prominent role in the policy towards Russia in all his functions, not only as Schröder's head of chancellery, but also later as foreign minister and federal president. Sigmar Gabriel was also responsible for many wrong decisions in the pipeline deals and in Russia policy in his roles as minister of economic affairs (2013–2017) and SPD chairman (2009–2017). After the annexation of Crimea, Gabriel repeatedly called for an end to sanctions against Russia and spoke of "civil war parties"[19] in Ukraine. Stephan Weil, the long-standing prime minister and SPD chairman of the state of Lower Saxony, spoke out explicitly against sanctions after the poisoning of the Russian opposition politician Alexei Navalny in the summer of 2020.[20] Gerhard Schröder rushed to publish his opinion that there were no reliable facts on the question of who was responsible for the poisoning of Navalny. It was then that Navalny described the former chancellor as "Putin's errand boy who protects murderers".[21] In the tense weeks leading up to the Russian attack on Ukraine on 24 February 2022, Schröder once again spoke out as a staunch Putin supporter and complained about the "Ukrainian sabre-rattling".[22]

Schröder has now been in the service of Russian companies for more than twice as long as he was chancellor.

In all these years, not a word of criticism of the Russian president has been heard from him. Despite public pressure and now also that from his party, he has not distanced himself from Putin. A few weeks after the start of the war, he even visited Putin in Moscow—allegedly to mediate. A second, private trip to Moscow followed a few months later, without any official announcement.

Recent news about Schröder confirms the ambivalence of the SPD's relationship with him: on 15 May 2023, the party's Federal Arbitration Commission finally rejected the applications of various local organisations that wanted to expel the former chancellor from the party. Putin's "best man" in Germany can thus remain in the SPD despite everything. And not only that: at the end of October 2023, he was even honoured for sixty years of SPD party membership at a ceremony in Hannover—with a golden badge of honour and a certificate signed by party leaders Saskia Esken and Lars Klingbeil.

However, it should not be forgotten that Schröder's Russia-friendly course was always enthusiastically supported by the Committee on Eastern European Economic Relations, which consists of six leading German business organisations and has more than three hundred member companies. The chairman from 2000 to 2010, Klaus Mangold, played a key role in the promotion of these contacts. He later worked as a highly paid lobbyist for the Orbán government in Hungary.

Not only the SPD, but also the Christian Democratic Union (CDU), which provided the federal chancellor for sixteen years, did not show much interest in reappraising Germany's Russia policy. In the 720 pages of the long-awaited memoirs of Angela Merkel,[23] there are no truly self-critical reflections about the blunder of her excessive reliance on Russian gas despite repeated warnings by Baltic and Polish politicians. A real reappraisal, including a massive increase of military expenditure, had to wait for the takeover by Friedrich Merz as federal chancellor of a CDU–SPD coalition government set up in May 2025.

While financial interests are likely to have played a much greater role for Gerhard Schröder than the continuation of the old policy of détente under new, completely changed circumstances, the attitude of other SPD politicians must be viewed in a more nuanced way. But, this does not alter the political responsibility of Steinmeier, Gabriel and certain still serving or retired prime ministers of some federal states. However, Steinmeier at least admitted his mistakes in Russia policy at Schloss Bellevue in April 2022: "My support for Nord Stream 2 was clearly a mistake. We held on to bridges that Russia no longer believed in and of which our partners had warned us. I had underestimated Putin's imperial mania. I was wrong, as were others."[24]

The habituation to political hypocrisy and nostalgia for the past in the oldest party of the largest state in the European Union has nevertheless remained strong even after its joining the coalition government headed by the strongly pro-Ukrainian CDU Chancellor Friedrich Merz. This was reflected in the so-called "peace mani-festo" in favour of a dialogue with Russia and against increased expenditures for arms, issued in June 2025 and signed by over one hundred Social Democrats, including several influential members of parliament.

5

YUGOSLAV WARS

THE BITTER CONSEQUENCES OF IGNORANCE

You cannot play the "song of freedom" on the instrument of violence.

Stanisław Jerzy Lec

Russia's war of aggression against Ukraine, with its unpredictable consequences, overshadows all other European problems. But from time to time, alarming headlines also report on the tension between Serbia and Kosovo and the danger of Bosnia-Herzegovina disintegrating as a result of the attempted secession of the Serb Republic (Republika Srpska). These messages then trigger warnings from Brussels and Washington, while international commentary fluctuates between trivialisation and dramatisation.

A quarter of a century after the Kosovo war, the time bombs are ticking again in the Balkans, and there can be no talk of lasting international crisis management in the name of European unification. Only two successor states to the disintegrated Yugoslavia have been accepted into the European Union: Slovenia in 2004 and Croatia in 2013. For the countries of the so-called Western Balkans, as Serbia, Bosnia, Kosovo, Macedonia, Montenegro and Albania are known in the misleading EU jargon, the EU made a solemn promise of accession at a summit meeting in Thessaloniki in June 2003. The prospect of EU membership was intended to act as an engine for democratisation and peace in both domestic and foreign policy in the countries of the region. With hopes of accession fading, hypocrisy now characterises the attitude of both sides: "Some pretend they want to enlarge, others pretend they want to join: That became the bitter formula for the relationship between Brussels and south-east Europe," noted the Balkan expert Norbert Mappes-Niediek in his comprehensive history of the Yugoslav Wars.[1]

In view of the continuing tensions in the Balkans and the particular threat to peace posed by Russian aggression, the question arises as to what lessons from the tragedy of the second Yugoslav state (1945–1991) are relevant to the conflicts of today. Did the EU and the United States—that is, the West—fail when Yugoslavia embarked on the path from disintegration to war, or was the scope for timely mediation or intervention minimal from the outset? In contrast to the collapse of the first Yugoslav state in 1941, this time the decisive impetus did not come from outside. It was a tragic paradox:

nobody in Europe wanted the Yugoslav multi-ethnic state to disintegrate, but nobody knew how the internal forces of destruction could be tamed.

The disintegration of Yugoslavia

Over the course of more than three decades, from Zagreb to Ljubljana, from Belgrade to Pristina and Skopje, I have got to know many people of different nationalities in the Balkans, including leading politicians and critical intellectuals. In my book on the communist Balkan states written at the end of the 1960s, the importance of nationalism was the central theme in describing the political and economic tensions between the six republics. Nevertheless, at that time I still believed that "the Yugoslavian unitary state, as much as it is plagued by tensions, exists and will continue to exist, because a secession of parts or a disintegration would expose the constituent nations to an even more endangered future".[2] In the 1980s, however, one could observe the creeping decline of the federal state as a result of the increasingly sharp conflicts over power and sinecures between the regional and national power elites. While travelling and at conferences in the second half of this decade, I witnessed the irreconcilable conflict between the Serbian centralist camp, led by Slobodan Milošević, and Slovenia, which advocated political pluralism and a market economy. I was present at the historic fourteenth party congress of the League of Communists of Yugoslavia in January 1990 when the Slovenian and Croatian delegations left the party congress. Thus, ten years after the death of the father figure Josip Broz Tito, the communist party, the most important bracket of the federal state, disappeared.

The explosives for Yugoslavia's self-destruction had been piling up for a long time and only needed to be ignited. The end of the federation was already sealed in the spring of 1989, when Milošević practically destroyed the balance of power within Yugoslavia by cancelling the autonomy of the provinces of Kosovo and Vojvodina, which belonged to Serbia. The declarations of independence by the parliaments of Slovenia and Croatia on 25 June 1991 marked the final end of the common state. A few days later, the first shots were fired when the Serb-controlled Yugoslav People's Army tried in vain to prevent Slovenia's independence by occupying the border crossings in the so-called Ten-Day War. This was the beginning of the series of bloody wars in Croatia, Bosnia and Kosovo, which only came to an end eight years later with the NATO air strikes against Serbia. The sad result of the violence can be seen in the statistics. In Bosnia, there were 102,100 fatalities—62 per cent Bosniaks, 25 per cent Serbs and 8 per cent Croats. Almost half died in the first year of the war in 1992. In Kosovo, 13,535 people were killed, missing or abducted at the end of the war years 1998–1999, including 10,588 of Albanian and 2,140 of Serbian nationality.[3] In addition, there were millions of refugees and displaced persons. From Kosovo alone, more than 800,000 people, almost half the population, were forced to leave their homes within a few weeks under Serbian pressure and were only able to return after the withdrawal of Serbian troops enforced by NATO. A description of the dramatic path from state collapse to war would go beyond the scope of this book.[4]

It was not the dry figures, but the films and documentaries, novels and diaries that reflected the extent of the violence during these wars. They raised the question: How could it happen that "normal" people behaved so inhumanely? How was it possible that people who had lived together as good neighbours for years became mortal enemies in a very short space of time and fought each other with unbelievable brutality? The course and details of the so-called ethnic cleansing are not the subject here. However, in view of its relevance today, the question arises as to why international politics reacted so half-heartedly and indecisively for so long. The outstanding Yugoslavia historian Holm Sundhaussen spoke the truth bluntly: "The role of the international community before, during and after the collapse of the state and the wars was shameful."[5]

The blindness of European politicians

As chance would have it, the intensification of the Yugoslavian state crisis coincided with the consequences of the *annus mirabilis*, the turning point of 1989. The end of the Cold War, the reunification of the two German states, the Gulf War and the dissolution of the Soviet Union overwhelmed diplomats and politicians. That the European Community and the United States in particular took a wait-and-see approach to developments in Yugoslavia was also due to the fact that the country was no longer regarded as a strategically important partner.

Two important factors are identical with regard to the wars in Yugoslavia at that time and Russia's current aggression against Ukraine: the United States played a decisive role in the Bosnian peace agreement of Dayton in 1995 and in the NATO air strikes against Serbia in 1999, just as it has supported Ukraine in its fight for survival after the Russian invasion until Donald Trump's second presidency. The numerous initiatives of the European Community at that time, just like those of the divided European Union, which has grown from twelve to twenty-seven members today, were characterised by a mixture of arrogance and ignorance. The British ambassador in Belgrade, Sir Peter Hall, said to his head of government, John Major, at the beginning of the Yugoslavian conflict: "Prime Minister, the first thing you need to know about these people is that they like to go round cutting each other's heads off." And the British foreign secretary Douglas Hurd declared in July 1991: "at the end of the day they [the peoples of Yugoslavia] have decided that they want a civil war. There will be a reproach to Europe, but we could not prevent it."[6] I heard astonishing stories about the ignorance of the people involved. The Austrian foreign minister Alois Mock, for example, told me that the French secretary general of the Council of Europe had asked him whether only Yugoslavian was spoken in Yugoslavia. And a well-known correspondent for the *New York Times* confused Slavonia (the heart of Croatia) with the state of Slovenia.

There was neither a uniform line nor considered ideas in the various negotiating initiatives of the then twelve heads of state and government of the European Community. They agreed, also with the United States, that the multi-ethnic state of Yugoslavia had to be preserved. Immediately after the reports of the first exchange of fire in Slovenia, the so-called troika (consisting of the foreign ministers of the previous, current and future European Community presidencies) was sent to Belgrade. These were Jacques Poos from Luxembourg, his predecessor Gianni De Michelis from Italy, and his successor Hans van den Broek from the Netherlands. Their offer was too small and came too late. The fact that the politicians acting as an improvised fire brigade were completely out of their depth is shown by their almost ridiculous and naive declarations. Jacques Poos, for example, announced confidently before departing for Belgrade: "This is Europe's hour, not the Americans'. If there is one problem that the Europeans can solve, it is the Yugoslavian one."[7] De Michelis even went so far as to claim after returning from Belgrade that the mere presence of "the rapid reaction force" of the three foreign ministers had caused the parties to the conflict to give in. I vividly remember the arrogance with which the Italian foreign minister treated the last Yugoslav foreign minister, Budimir Lončar, and the Austrian foreign minister, Alois Mock, during a special programme on ORF Oststudio in 1991, masking his ignorance of the true causes of the state crisis behind grandiose phrases.

It must be emphasised, however, that the US secretary of state James Baker rejected any intervention in a much-quoted speech on 21 June 1991 during a lightning trip to Belgrade and spoke out in favour of the survival of the state of Yugoslavia. European Commission president Jacques Delors and Council president Jacques Santer made similarly clear statements against the independence of Slovenia and Croatia. In the phase of open warfare, clear differences emerged between reunified Germany and France, and the international players sent different signals to the parties to the conflict. The Greater Serbian warmonger Slobodan Milošević skilfully exploited all of this for years to divide the international community.

Norbert Mappes-Niediek aptly notes that the attempts to preserve Yugoslavia were wrong from the outset: "The Western statesmen came to Yugoslavia like an angry mother entering the nursery: as an authority figure who is too annoyed to get involved in the background of the trivial details of the quarrels."[8] In an arrogant speech to the assembled representatives of the Yugoslav conflict parties on 30 June 1991, European Commission minister Hans van den Broek declared that this crisis could be easily resolved with political will. Mappes-Niediek commented: "But what had triggered the crisis, what the motives of the conflicting parties were: None of that was his concern."

After the failure of the major international Yugoslavia conference in September 1991, the German government decided to recognise Slovenia and Croatia on its own on 23 December. This triggered fierce debates. The other European Community member states followed suit on 15 January 1992, and in my comments I also always spoke out in favour of recognising the two states, despite the possible consequences in Bosnia-Herzegovina. The fact is that Milošević and the army leadership interpreted the Western declarations against the division of Yugoslavia as an incentive for their offensives. However, it was not the recognition that triggered the acts of war, but the other way round: it was the violent actions of the Serbs, the army and the Serbian paramilitary gangs in Croatia that accelerated the policy of recognition. A key role was played by German foreign minister Hans-Dietrich Genscher, who defended the recognition of Croatia and Slovenia in his memoirs: "Ending the aggression against and in Croatia, averting the danger of new aggression against Slovenia, that had to be the primary goal—and it was achieved. What is there to criticise about that?"[9] As chairman of the Conference on Security and Cooperation in Europe (the OSCE), he had repeatedly contacted the leaders of the republics personally and always acted in cooperation with the other EU powers. His blue jacket and yellow jumper were a favourite subject for photographers and TV cameras.

The role of the United States

The United States stayed out of the Yugoslavian wars for a long time. Two personalities in Bill Clinton's administration, the UN ambassador Madeleine Albright and the deputy secretary of state Strobe Talbott, both profound experts on Eastern Europe, were primarily responsible for the Americans taking the reins after two years of failed peace efforts by the UN and the EU. As so often in the history of the Yugoslav Wars, a mass murder, this time by a mortar shell fired by the Serbian besiegers on the market square in Sarajevo on 5 February 1994, marked the turning point. After the deaths of sixty-eight passers-by, NATO issued an ultimatum to the Serbian army: it was to withdraw its heavy weapons from the positions around the city. At the end of February, US fighter-bombers shot down four Serbian aircraft that had flouted the flight ban and dropped bombs over Bosnia.

The surrender of the Dutch blue helmet soldiers at Srebrenica in Bosnia to the Serbian soldiers of Radovan

Karadžić and General Ratko Mladić led to the killing of 8,372 Bosnian men and boys between the ages of 12 and 77 in July 1995. The genocide of Srebrenica was the largest war crime in Europe since the Second World War. Only four weeks later, after the reconquest of western Slavonia by the Croatian army, 200,000 Serbs were expelled from Krajina, where their ancestors had been settled by Empress Maria Theresa in the eighteenth century.

The main architect of the negotiations leading to the Dayton Peace Agreement in November 1995 was Richard Holbrooke, assistant secretary of state at the US State Department, who immortalised his success in a 600-page book.[10] The following excerpt will suffice to assess his detached brand of "international psychology": "The Serbs were obstinate and liked to run their mouths. But if you called their bluff and put a gun to their head, they were ultimately just little bullies. In recent years, the West had made the mistake of treating the Serbs as if they were rational people with whom it was possible to have serious discussions, negotiate sensibly and reach a binding agreement. In fact, however, they responded only to force, or at least the unmistakable and credible threat that it would be used."[11] George Packer's biography of Holbrooke vividly describes how difficult the process was even in the US bureaucracy and how hesitant and divided the European states were in the decision-making process.[12]

The "betrayal of the intellectuals"

Not only Holbrooke but almost all politicians and diplomats who were involved in the Yugoslav Wars wrote memoirs to justify themselves and accuse their rivals of failings. I would like to describe here some examples of the hypocrisy and unscrupulous change of heart of well-known writers, scientists and journalists during the eight years of the Yugoslav Wars. This is what Julien Benda called the "betrayal of intellectuals" in his famous book in 1927: "The cause for which the *clercs* [that is, scholars, experts, highly educated people, intellectuals, artists and philosophers, lawyers and journalists] committed their betrayal at that time was primarily that of the nation." National sentiment became national pride and national resentment, warned Benda, adding the timeless words that were confirmed every day in Bosnia: "Incidentally, the fact that, contrary to common opinion, pride is a stronger passion than interest quickly becomes clear when you see how people are killed far more often because their pride has been hurt than because their interests have been damaged."[13]

Perhaps the saddest example I know of the modern *clerc*, the intellectual turncoat, comes from first-hand experience in the former Yugoslavia. In the summer of 1967, I met some critical Yugoslav philosophers and sociologists such as Mihailo Marković, Svetozar Stojanović and others on the picturesque Adriatic island of Korčula at the international summer school organised by the journal *Praxis*. In the years that followed, the *Praxis* authors, who also became well-known abroad, wrote numerous courageous essays against the Yugoslav Communist Party's total monopoly on power and advocated the idea of a humanistic Marxism against nationalism. For example, Mihailo Marković wrote in 1975: "The national bureaucracy is trying to arouse the political interest of apathetic workers and peasants by mobilising grassroots forces for distinctly national goals, to spread a veil of oblivion over the real social problems, to make itself the leading force of a real mass movement. The usual strategy of creating a nationalist movement consists of fuelling hatred against another nation, the 'main culprit', on the one hand, and nurturing self-pity for one's own nation, the 'main victim', on the other. Once the bureaucracy has taken the initiative, a whole army of national-minded economists, statisticians, historians and journalists take on the task of digging up the relevant one-sided data and views and hammering them into people's brains."[14]

The journal *Praxis* was discontinued in 1975 after a political row and the cancellation of subsidies. Marković, whom I had also met a few times in his flat in Belgrade, later lost his position at the Faculty of Philosophy at Belgrade University, along with several other professors. Although he was invited by prestigious US universities, he was not given a passport. On the occasion of an ORF

TV interview with Serbian prime minister Ivan Stambolić, I intervened to support Marković's (repeatedly rejected) exit permit, arguing that the travel ban would probably do more harm to Yugoslavia's reputation than anything Marković would say in his lectures. Incidentally, he was later allowed to leave the country.

I was all the more surprised when Marković turned out to be one of the main authors of the notorious nationalist memorandum of the Serbian Academy of Sciences in 1986. This much-praised philosopher of "humanistic Marxism" became the most eloquent and unrestrained defender of the Milošević regime and the war as vice president of the successor organisation to the former Communist Party, which was renamed the Socialist Party. In an interview with the London weekly *The Economist*, for example, he said: "The war and the economic chaos will continue until all Serbs are united in one state."[15]

Another friend, the "*praxis*" philosopher Svetozar Stojanović, had also repeatedly warned of the "corruption of intellectuals through entry into the hierarchy" as a "great danger" and criticised the "apologetic intellectuals". During an ORF Club 2 discussion about Yugoslavia in the autumn of 1988, I was already increasingly uncomfortable with the fact that Stojanović, who spoke fluent German, repeatedly avoided taking a clear stand in favour of equal rights for Kosovo Albanians by using general phrases.

It was therefore no longer so surprising to me that Stojanović became an advisor and interpreter to Dobrica Ćosić, the literary godfather of Serbian nationalism, when he took office as president of the so-called Federal Republic of Yugoslavia (consisting only of Serbia and Montenegro) in 1992. Stojanović justified Serbian nationalism in speeches at numerous Western universities, where he had previously worked as a visiting professor.

Politician with courage

Bogdan Bogdanović, the former mayor of Belgrade, an internationally recognised architect and essayist, was a courageous opponent of nationalist propaganda based on myths, self-pity and aggression. However, with his prophetic concern for Serbia's fate, with his stand against "irretrievable self-destruction, self-destruction through panic fear of the other and the others", he remained a lone voice in the wilderness.[16] After the outbreak of the Yugoslav Wars and as a result of a wave of threats, he went into exile in Vienna in good time.

Two leading Serbian politicians, whom I had the honour of meeting while they were still in their official positions, were less fortunate. As already mentioned, I had a TV interview with the prime minister of Serbia, Ivan Stambolić, in the early 1980s. Coming from a prominent communist family, Stambolić had always supported Slobodan Milošević, who was several years younger than him, more than anyone else and "loved him like a brother".[17] As Stambolić was an opponent of the Serbian nationalists and a supporter of Titoist consensus politics, Milošević swept his patron out of all positions as early as 1987. Even though disempowered, Stambolić remained a latent threat to Milošević as a possible opponent in the presidential election in autumn 2000. In the summer of 2000, Stambolić disappeared while jogging in a Belgrade park. The remains of his body were found almost three years later in a lime pit in Vojvodina during the investigation into the murder of Zoran Djindjić. Serbian secret police had murdered him, presumably on Milošević's instructions to the head of the secret service and the interior minister.

Zoran Djindjić, prime minister of Serbia from 2001 to 2003, was the most courageous and unusual Serbian politician of the late twentieth and early twenty-first centuries. I had already got to know him as a young member of the opposition. Djindjić, who had studied in Tübingen, often appeared on ORF, and we met several times for background discussions and interviews. He made Serbian and European history twice. First in autumn 2000, when he prepared and carried out the overthrow of Milošević in cold blood and with brilliance. In a conversation lasting several hours in Vienna, he described the details of this "revolution with elements of a secret organisation" to me.[18] And then, in June 2001, he made the fateful decision to hand over the arrested Milošević to the UN war crimes tribunal in The Hague.[19] Shortly after I met him for the last time at the Salzburg Eastern Europe Congress of the World Economic Forum in 2002, Djindjić was murdered by members of a criminal network on 12 March 2003.

In the two decades that followed, there was no Serbian politician far and wide who could have replaced the determined, lightning-quick and charismatic Djindjić. This vacuum of credibility at the apex of power is so dangerous because the situation in Serbia was and is of central importance for the long-term stabilisation of the Balkan region. Under Serbia's current "strongman", President Aleksandar Vučić, all the stops are still being pulled out of a large-scale Serbian, nationalist and racist propaganda programme: an always explosive mixture of myths, aggression and feelings of revenge. And just as thirty years ago, a hypocrisy characterised by domestic political and personal power interests continues to determine the policy of the divided EU in the Balkans, where time bombs are still ticking from Serbia to Kosovo, from Bosnia to North Macedonia.

The warning of the great British historian Arnold Toynbee (1889–1975) applies more than ever to this volatile corner of the Balkans: "No one is in a position to guarantee that everyone is immune to every temptation. Under certain conditions, the volcano may erupt, even if its fire has been dormant for so long that it is thought to be extinguished."[20]

6

THE BALKANS

PLAYGROUND FOR WESTERN HYPOCRITES

Reality can be changed, fiction must be invented anew.

Stanisław Jerzy Lec

If one asks why the European Union has lost its credibility in the Balkan countries, the focus today is no longer on its failure to prevent the Yugoslav Wars (1991–1999), but above all on the disappointment over the broken promises made by the solemn Thessaloniki Declaration in 2003. At that time, Albania, Bosnia-Herzegovina, Kosovo, Macedonia, Montenegro and Serbia were promised EU membership.[1] The arguments made to justify their continued exclusion, referring to the lack of rule of law, corruption or restricted press freedom, are only one side of the coin. The other side is a mixture of indifference, appeasement and hypocrisy that has characterised the Balkan policy of Western leaders from Angela Merkel to Emmanuel Macron over the last two decades.

Courageous North Macedonia

The small Republic of North Macedonia offers particularly notable examples of this. Let's take a brief historical look back. The tripartition of the strategically important Macedonia in the two Balkan Wars of 1912–1913 (it was roughly the size of Bavaria at the time) did not lead to lasting peace. Macedonia was mainly divided between Greece and Serbia, while Bulgaria only received 10 per cent of the territory it coveted. The Macedonian question remained a bone of contention in the interwar period, often a powder keg, between Bulgarians, Serbs and Greeks. In all three countries, the national movements of the Macedonian Slavs were suppressed. The picture changed abruptly when post-war Yugoslavia came into being.

The creation of a Macedonian republic within the Yugoslav federation set a new development in motion. I regularly visited the capital Skopje before and after the massive earthquake of 26 July 1963, as well as other parts of the country. Thanks to my close relationship with the leading Macedonian politician Kiro Gligorov,[2] I was able to observe and describe the development of Macedonia and the process of its inhabitants becoming a nation while it was still part of the Yugoslav republic. It was thanks to Gligorov, the first president of the independent state from 1991, that Macedonia did not become directly involved in the Yugoslav Wars of the

1990s. From the very beginning, however, there were not only conflicts with its difficult neighbours Greece and Bulgaria, but also tensions with the large Albanian minority, which make up a quarter of the two million inhabitants.

The international response to the Macedonian state since independence in 1991 has become a prime case study of the ethnic nationalism of Greece and Bulgaria as well as hypocritical appeasement on the part of France and Germany. The United Nations was only allowed to admit the new state as a member in 1993 under the provisional name Former Yugoslav Republic of Macedonia, while accession to NATO and the path to negotiations with the EU failed due to the veto of Greece, which even imposed a trade blockade on its small neighbour in 1994–1995.

The main bone of contention was the original state name, Republic of Macedonia, which, according to the Greeks, indicated a Macedonian claim to the Greek province of the same name. For twenty-seven years, all Greek governments blocked the western integration of the Republic of Macedonia. The fall of the nationalist prime minister Nikola Gruevski in 2016 after ten years of unbridled enrichment, the change of government in 2017, and pressure from the EU, with a personal appearance by German Chancellor Angela Merkel in Skopje in 2018 in favour of a compromise, finally opened the way to an agreement on the name Republic of North Macedonia.

Although legally sentenced to two years in prison for corruption, in November 2018 Gruevski managed to flee to Hungary, where his old friend Viktor Orbán immediately granted him political asylum. Despite Gruevski's intrigues and the protests of radical nationalists in both countries, the Greek and Macedonian parliaments voted in favour of the renaming, putting an end to a decades-long name dispute.

However, the peace agreement between Athens and Skopje, which was so actively promoted by the EU, soon turned out to be a deceptive success for the Macedonians. French President Emmanuel Macron, who, according to the author Sylvain Prudhomme, "offended the French with his arrogance, his haughtiness, his condescension",[3] caused confusion and resentment not only in NATO and EU policy, but also in the Balkans with his erratic solo efforts. In contrast to the official policy of the EU Commission, France has become the biggest opponent of EU enlargement in recent years and has threatened to undermine the EU line. In October 2019, the French government officially vetoed the start of accession negotiations with North Macedonia and Albania, even though the two countries have fulfilled all the conditions and are considered a model for reform efforts in the region.

Florian Bieber, head of the Centre for South-Eastern Europe at the University of Graz, rightly condemned the French move as a blow to the EU's credibility. For twenty years, European policy has held out the prospect of integration with the EU in return for strengthening the rule of law, democracy and the resolution of open conflicts, said Bieber, adding: "If North Macedonia does not even receive the modest 'reward' of accession talks despite the difficult and domestically courageous step of resolving the name dispute with Greece, why should Serbia seek a compromise with Kosovo, why should political elites limit their own power and strengthen the rule of law?"[4]

The confusing solo efforts of Emmanuel Macron

It was not only in Brussels and the Balkans that people shook their heads at Macron's open departure from the common EU line. From Berlin to Washington, he lost much of his credibility with some half-baked and premature ideas. When, following his visit to Beijing in spring 2023, he called for the Europeans to be more cautious in the Taiwan conflict between China and the United States, this sparked outrage both within the EU and in Washington. In a press conference on the flight back from Beijing, Macron explained: "The worst thing would be to think that we Europeans will become followers on this issue and either have to follow the American rhythm or a Chinese overreaction"; Europe runs the risk of being dragged into crises "that may not be ours". Macron had managed to turn his trip to

China into a PR coup for the Chinese president and a foreign policy disaster for Europe, wrote German foreign policy expert Norbert Röttgen of the Christian Democratic Union on Twitter (X), adding that an attack on Taiwan would become all the more likely the more Xi Jinping believed that Europe would remain neutral in such a conflict.[5]

With his victories in two presidential elections, Emmanuel Macron—after Charles de Gaulle—was considered the most successful political career changer in French history. However, charismatic leaders in a parliamentary democracy are only above contradictions as long as they prove themselves through miracles and successes. In contrast to Angela Merkel during her sixteen years as chancellor with a formative role in the European Union, President Macron has repeatedly lacked the last two of the three qualities that, according to the sociologist Max Weber, characterise a politician—passion, a sense of responsibility and a sense of proportion—in domestic and foreign policy. Two weeks after his five-hour meeting with President Vladimir Putin in Moscow and the latter's promise to exercise "restraint", Russian tanks rolled across the Ukrainian border. Macron's much-publicised mediation project turned out to be a castle in the air.

Above all, Macron was unable to regain the credibility destroyed by his *Economist* interview in November 2019. In this interview, he described NATO as "brain dead", saw the EU on the brink of the abyss, and at the same time called for a "new, strategic dialogue" with Moscow.[6] He and Viktor Orbán understood the Russia issue in a similar way, it was said, and perhaps Orbán would succeed in convincing the Visegrád Group of Central European countries and Poland in particular of their common view. However, at a working lunch in Paris in March 2023, Macron was able to discuss the mood in the Kremlin rather than in Warsaw with Orbán, the Russian dictator's best European friend. Poland is now seen as a frontline state directly threatened by Russia and is also supported in its critical stance towards Russia by the Czech Republic, but not by Orbán's Hungary. Macron's ambivalence, impatience and unpredictability in his quest for leadership have weakened the unity of the EU and strengthened Russia's position.

Despite massive criticism from diplomats and commentators following his missteps on the global political stage, the hyperactive Macron performed another, at least rhetorical about-turn on Balkan policy in spring 2023 after four years of obstruction. In a speech to the international security forum Globsec Bratislava, the president redefined France's position on Eastern Europe and the Balkans. After referring to the suppression of the Hungarian uprising by Soviet Russia in 1956, he admitted that the history and painful memories of the Eastern Europeans had not always been sufficiently recognised or listened to. The president emphasised that France could be counted on. With regard to his infamous statement in November 2019 about the "brain death" of NATO, he also showed "almost self-criticism", according to observers, by claiming that President Putin had "shaken up the alliance with the worst of all electric shocks".[7]

However, with his erratic behaviour and his tendency to go it alone, Macron has smashed so much china that it is questionable whether he will ever be able to regain the initial capital of trust through rhetorical rectifications. There have been other hypocrites in the history of the EU, but Macron still plays a prominent role thanks to his rhetorical talent and his undisguised desire for recognition. It remains to be seen to what extent the rumours[8] are true that the French veto (from 2019) of the start of EU accession negotiations with North Macedonia encouraged neighbouring Bulgaria to impose an EU veto on the government in Skopje.

Bulgarian megalomania

For Bulgaria, the Macedonian question was and is politically explosive. The creation and further development of the Yugoslav Republic of Macedonia became the hated symbol of a historical defeat from the very beginning. The Bulgarians, whom Bismarck had described as "the Prussians of the Balkans", became involved in two Balkan wars and two world wars between 1912 and

1944 in order to regain the territories of Macedonia and Thrace that had been promised to them in the peace treaty of San Stefano in 1878 and that were lost again at the Congress of Berlin in the same year. The longing for the borders that would have made Bulgaria the largest state in the Balkans after the "liberation of the lost territories" dominated Bulgarian politics until the end of the Second World War. This national myth led to the alliance with Hitler's Germany and the temporary occupation of territories in Yugoslavia and Greece.

The Republic of Macedonia in the Yugoslav federation was already an enemy of Bulgaria during the communist era. Even during my repeated trips to the country, which was still communist at the time, I always felt that my expectations had been betrayed. After a tour of so-called Pirin Macedonia in south-west Bulgaria, I spent hours arguing with journalists and writers who tried to convince me that there could not be a Macedonian nation because the Macedonians— wherever they were—were simply Bulgarians. "We are the strongest nation in the Balkans!" the editor-in-chief of the local communist newspaper in Veliko Tarnovo, once the capital of the Second Bulgarian Empire in the Middle Ages, told me as we watched the young cadets from the officers' school march past. "No other nation was under Turkish rule for five hundred years and yet managed to preserve its national identity, language and traditions intact."

After the Greeks had ended their years-long blockade by changing the name of the neighbouring country to North Macedonia, the Bulgarian nationalists went into action: they demanded constitutional changes to recognise a Bulgarian minority and drastic changes to the national identity and language of the Macedonians. Bulgaria, one of the most corrupt and politically unstable countries in the EU, is blocking North Macedonia, even though this country has carried out credible reforms and was granted candidate status back in 2005. The pressure exerted behind the scenes by the governments in Berlin and Paris and by the EU Commission in favour of a foul compromise by amending the constitution turned out to be a boomerang. The Macedonians, who have been repeatedly let down by the EU, voted with a massive majority in favour of returning the nationaliust VMRO to power at the presidential and parliamentary elections in May 2024. The latent tensions between the Macedonian majority and the strong Albanian minority also threaten the deceptive domestic political calm. The national megalomania supported by Moscow in Bulgaria and the EU's concession to make this bilateral dispute part of the accession negotiations expose the hypocrisy of Western symbolic politics with regard to the countries of the so-called Western Balkans.

Greater Serbian nationalism

Serbia continues to play a key role in this context. The war crimes trial against Serbian President Slobodan

Milošević began more than two decades ago, and he died in his cell in The Hague in 2006 without being sentenced. However, his highly dangerous ideas, which plunged Yugoslavia into war and misery, remain alive. His nationalist goal of a "Greater Serbia", that is, a common state in which all Serbs live together, has once again become socially acceptable under the slogan "Serbian World". According to the argument, the Serbian government must take care of its compatriots in neighbouring countries, especially in Kosovo and Bosnia-Herzegovina, but also in Croatia and Montenegro, in order to prevent them from being disadvantaged there.

President Aleksandar Vučić, who served the evil Milošević regime as information minister at the age of 28, has remained a staunch Greater Serbian nationalist despite his flexible tactics throughout his career. He is accused of threatening in the Belgrade parliament in July 1995 that Serbia would kill a hundred Muslims for every Serb killed. Even though he distanced himself from such "stupidities" and "mistakes" in 2008, Vučić has continued to pursue a nationalist course as head of government and, since 2017, as president, combined with an increasingly conspicuous see-saw policy between the EU and the "brothers" Russia and China. He is said to have met Russian President Vladimir Putin, who is still considered the most popular foreign politician in Serbia, twelve times. Although Serbia condemned the Russian war of aggression against Ukraine at the UN, it did not support the sanctions. The mood in Serbia was characterised by the unbelievable initial reaction of the pro-regime media. Two days before the Russian invasion, the tabloid *Informer* reported verbatim on its front page: "The Americans are plunging the world into chaos. Ukraine has attacked Russia!"[9]

According to the independent NGO Freedom House, Serbia has become an "only partially free state" under Vučić's government.[10] With his power clique and extensive network, he controls the secret service, the corrupt administration and the media. The public media are treated as his private property. Before the last presidential election, Vučić made 300 full-length TV appearances in 2021 alone. He always presents himself as the saviour of the Serbs, enjoys the benefits of nepotism, and even cultivates contacts with the underworld.[11] Vučić rules almost at will. Hate slogans are spread in the media under his control. The huge murals painted on building facades of the "Butcher of the Balkans", Ratko Mladić, who was sentenced to life imprisonment; the allegations of "victor's justice" against Serbia; and the spread of lies about the mass murder in Srebrenica show how strong historical revisionism is.

The powder keg of northern Kosovo

Against this political and ideological backdrop, it is understandable that Vučić plays the Kosovo card whenever the pressure at home increases. What is at stake? The former autonomous Serbian province was initially administered by a UN mission following the NATO intervention and the withdrawal of Serbian troops in 1999. In 2008, the Kosovan parliament proclaimed the independence of the Republic of Kosovo. To date, 117 of the 193 UN member states have recognised the Republic of Kosovo, not including five EU member states with their own minority problems: Spain, Greece, Romania, Slovakia and Cyprus.

Why is the fate of Kosovo, where Serbs make up only around 5 per cent of the population (91 per cent are Albanians), so important for Serbia? For many Serbs, the battle lost against the Ottomans on the Field of Blackbirds in Kosovo in June 1389 has remained an identity-forming myth. The old Serbian monasteries are located there, and the Field of Blackbirds is considered the cradle of Serbianism. The Serbian writer Bora Ćosić describes it as "a narrow-minded mythomaniac version", according to which the Serbs "believe that they are registered in the eternal land registers as the sole owners of this land [...] The Serbs also tend to make an epic out of their defeats."[12]

Vučić uses all of this for regularly recurring threats to use Kosovo as a fuse to detonate the powder keg. The conflict is primarily about northern Kosovo, the predominantly Serb-inhabited northern region. Despite repeated negotiations under international supervision, no real progress has ever been made. With the appointment of Albin Kurti, the former student leader and political prisoner in the Milošević era, as prime minister in 2020–2021, a personally unblemished but deeply nationalist politician came to power in Kosovo. Kurti demands access to international organisations such as the United Nations. In return, the government of Kosovo should grant the Serb minority the right to self-administration and allow municipalities with a Serb majority to form an association. This was promised back in 2013 by the Kosovo leadership at the time, but has not yet been realised. Kurti is now calling for Kosovo to be recognised before an association of Serb municipalities can be created.

In spring 2023, a Franco-German initiative along the lines of the compromise between the Federal Republic of Germany and the GDR appeared to have achieved a breakthrough. Serbia would not recognise Kosovo under international law, but would not raise any objections to Kosovo's membership of international organisations. Both sides should recognise each other's national symbols, including passports, car registration plates and customs stamps. In return, Kosovo should finally allow the creation of an association of Serb municipalities. However, the success celebrated by the EU Commission remained just a piece of paper; new, dangerous clashes broke out in northern Kosovo in May 2023. Serb militias attacked the NATO-led KFOR peacekeepers and injured thirty NATO soldiers.[13]

Abysmal mistrust continues to prevail between the leaderships in Belgrade and Pristina. There are repeated provocations, and the game of fire on both sides can spiral out of control at any time. Vučić regularly runs aggressive media campaigns against Kosovo; he called Kurti "terrorist scum"; and he has never really agreed to a deal with Kosovo. Independent observers believe that he wants to annex northern Kosovo, an area that has never really been integrated into the Kosovan state in the past twenty-four years.[14] It is also widely believed that the attack by an organised criminal group on the Kosovan police in September 2023 in northern Kosovo was organised from Belgrade. The Serb terrorists, heavily armed and dressed like soldiers, shot and killed a police officer. These provocations sparked outrage in the EU. Incidentally, two days before the attack on the Kosovar police, Serbian foreign minister Ivica Dačić and Russian foreign minister Sergei Lavrov met for a friendly dialogue.[15]

Independent observers emphasise that Western diplomacy has been partly to blame for the escalation owing to its policy of appeasement towards Serbia. They stressed the urgent need for an about-turn in policy towards President Vučić if the situation was not to risk becoming even more dangerous. The EU should freeze funds for the country and consider cancelling the Schengen visa-free regime for Serbian citizens in the event of further escalation.[16]

The geopolitical consequences

The geopolitical consequences of the war in Ukraine are also reflected in the Balkans, particularly in Kosovo and Bosnia. Moscow has always supported Serbia on the issue of recognising Kosovo as a state. For Russia, the flare-up in northern Kosovo as well as in Bosnia is a strategic advantage. Milorad Dodik, the strongman at the head of Republika Srpska, the Serb state within the Federation of Bosnia-Herzegovina, is a close associate of the Russian president. He regularly visits Putin, even after the invasion of Ukraine.

The extremely nationalist president of Republika Srpska has repeatedly threatened the secession of its 1.2 million inhabitants and hinted at unification with Serbia. Vučić had already warned that a huge and serious crisis was brewing in Bosnia. After the end of the Bosnian War in 1995, 60,000 NATO soldiers ensured that the Dayton Peace Agreement was enforced. Today, the EU-led peacekeeping mission has only 1,100 soldiers. Dodik now no longer wants to recognise the decisions of the high representative for Bosnia and Herzegovina appointed by the international community, currently the German Christian Schmidt. Dodik can escalate tensions as required and completely undermine Schmidt's reputation with constant crossfire. This conflict, co-fuelled by Moscow, could lead to the dangerous break-up of the shaky federation of Bosniak-Croat and Serb entities.

An interesting new player in Balkan politics is Hungarian prime minister Viktor Orbán. A friend of Putin and critic of EU sanctions against Russia, he maintains close contacts with both Vučić and Dodik and is a vocal supporter of Serbia's accession to the European Union. He met demonstratively with Dodik on several occasions and granted Republika Srpska a loan of 100 million euros in 2021. Hungary would prevent EU sanctions against Dodik, which the European Parliament has repeatedly called for. In this situation, Olivér Várhelyi from Hungary, the EU commissioner responsible for enlargement and neighbourhood policy from 2019 to 2024, played a controversial role behind the scenes. Prior to his appointment, he was head of the Hungarian representation to the EU and is considered a loyal follower of his prime minister. With his appointment, Commission president Ursula von der Leyen, who owed her election to the Polish and Hungarian votes, made a serious mistake.

Whatever one may think of the stubbornness and persistence of Albin Kurti, the prime minister of Kosovo, in implementing his demands, it must be emphasised that Vučić and Kurti were judged according to double standards in Brussels and also in Washington until recently. In the early summer of 2023, for example, punitive measures were imposed on the Kosovo government by both the EU and the United States because it wanted to prevent the *de facto* partition of the state by all means (including controversial ones). All serious observers point out how lenient the United States and the EU have been with Vučić in comparison. Years ago, German Chancellor Angela Merkel praised "Serbia's path of reforms"[17] during a visit by Vučić to Berlin. Despite his dismal domestic political record, the Serbian president has succeeded in making the West believe that he is an irreplaceable stabilising factor. Neither the EU nor the United States has a plan for a fundamental solution to the Kosovo conflict. As the US expert on Eastern Europe Janusz Bugajski has noted, Western politicians believe that they can turn political leaders like Vučić into democrats by working together. Five years ago, the journalist Aleks Eror wrote a sarcastic article about how Western heads of state and government were courting Vučić as a regional anchor of stability.[18] Since the war in Ukraine, the aim has obviously been to prevent him from slipping any further towards Russia. Whether this calculation is correct remains doubtful. The Serbian head of state is already trying to divert attention from internal tensions by agitating against Kosovo and backing Dodik's divisive course in Bosnia. Russia, Turkey and China are also capitalising on the disappointment caused by the ongoing weakening of the EU presence in the Balkans and the paralysis of US policy in the Balkans to assert their own national interests in Bosnia.

The contradictory policies of the EU and the United States towards the successor states of Yugoslavia are characterised by a mixture of ignorance, indifference and hypocrisy. Whether the EU can ever regain its geopolitical credibility in the region remains to be seen. The demonstratively close contacts that Vučić maintains with the autocrats in Moscow, Beijing and Budapest could provoke a serious crisis in the Balkans in the slipstream of the Ukraine war and the Middle East conflict.

7

VIKTOR ORBÁN

THE WORLD CHAMPION OF CYNICISM

One can also be a virtuoso of the foul game.

Stanisław Jerzy Lec

The Hungarian prime minister Viktor Orbán can be justly regarded as the most famous and infamous Hungarian politician in contemporary history. As leader of the Fidesz party, he won the parliamentary elections four times between 2010 and 2022, always with a two-thirds majority of seats. Orbán skilfully exploited the majority-favouring electoral system to rule out any subsequent possibility of an opposition victory. Through a series of lightning-fast decisions, he successfully eliminated the protection of the rule of law enshrined in the constitution. His government established a firm grip over the Constitutional Court and the public prosecutor's office, the public media and the central bank. A new constitution, now amended fifteen times according to political expediency, and constant adjustments to the electoral law have weakened and divided the opposition parties, which *de facto* no longer have access to the mass media and advertising space.

The sociologist Bálint Magyar has called the system that has been built up in Hungary over fifteen years "a post-communist mafia state ruled by the political-economic clan of Prime Minister Viktor Orbán", while the political scientist Vilmos Körösényi invented the term "leader democracy". The best description of the Orbán regime may be the one written by the philosopher Ágnes Heller (1929–2019): "A tyranny that is rubber-stamped in elections every four years. It relies on a clientele that has become rich and whose loyalty is bought. Its mass appeal is due to its extremist ideology. Its elements are racist nationalism, the production of enemy images, the creation of a sense of threat, the permanent fight against something and someone who wants to destroy Hungary, with Orbán as the protector and saviour. The soul of the people is poisoned with hatred and fear."[1]

All of this happened in the glare of the international media; every important step in the liquidation of liberal democracy was documented in detail and criticised. After all, Hungary has been a member state of NATO (since 1999) and the European Union (since 2004). How was it then possible for the Orbán government even as late as 2024 to water down EU sanctions on

Russia, to delay with its veto financial and military aid for Ukraine, and even to take over the rotating presidency of the EU on 1 July 2024 for six months? The reason is not just the structural weakness of the twenty-seven-member organisation due to the requirement of consensus when taking decisions over important issues. From the very beginning of European integration, personalities—from French President Charles de Gaulle to German Chancellor Angela Merkel—have also played an important role. Though Hungary is a small land-locked Central European country of less than ten million people, Viktor Orbán has managed to emerge hand in hand with Russian President Vladimir Putin as a key destroyer of European values and unity.

Orbán is indeed one of those virtuosos of the false game who are unashamedly proud of their mastery of hypocrisy. In the course of my work on his biography, I discovered a treacherous, because improvised, remark in a recording of a speech delivered on 31 May 2012 before a select audience of committed supporters, describing his tactics towards the EU as a "peacock dance". How can one fool critics in the EU's governing bodies so adroitly that they get the (false) impression that the Hungarian side has given in, even though it continues to pursue the Orbán course unswervingly? Orbán explains: "Because of the dance rules of diplomacy, we have to present the rejection as if we want to make friends with them. This dance involves nodding our heads in agreement with two or three of the seven proposals (we had already made them anyway, they just didn't realise it) and rejecting the remaining two, which we don't want, so that we actually accept the majority. This complicated game is a kind of peacock dance." An unprecedented public yet presumptuous confession that shows how simple-minded opponents are being hoodwinked by the Hungarian grandmaster without realising it. This improvised remark is now missing from the authorised text of his speech.[2]

Personal encounters with Viktor Orbán

In view of Orbán's political importance, a few words may therefore be appropriate about our personal encounters and my impressions of him. I met him first through a chain of coincidences at the beginning of his political career and for the last time on the eve of his greatest and decisive triumph. Our first meeting took place on 22 September 1993. He was then 33 years old, leading Fidesz, the smallest party in the Hungarian parliament, delivering a speech in not very polished English followed by a discussion at the Institute for Human Sciences (IWM) in Vienna. Afterwards, I talked to him about the political situation in Hungary at an intimate dinner organised by the Polish director of the institute, Krzysztof Michalski. He impressed me not only with his frankness about his rivalry with Gábor Fodor[3] for the leadership of the Fidesz party, but also with his liberal stance in opposition to the nationalist, right-wing conservative course of the Antall government. He conveyed to me, the audience and his hosts the image of a promising, progressive politician of the young generation. He was even vice president of the Liberal International at the time and proudly hosted the Liberal World Conference in Budapest in autumn 1993.

Six years later I met a profoundly changed, self-confident Viktor Orbán, as prime minister since 1998, the youngest in Europe at that time and by then a champion of a nationalist and right-wing conservative course. He gave a speech on 6 June 1999 at the International Europe Forum in Göttweig Abbey in Lower Austria on Hungary and its European policy. Having been since its beginnings moderator of this annual conference, I also introduced him with a few sentences. Over lunch, hosted by Lower Austria's governor, Erwin Pröll, we toasted our switching to the more intimate "you" in conversation with a glass of wine, Hungarian style, and I congratulated him on the fact that—unlike former Hungarian president Árpád Göncz and other prominent speakers—he had restrained himself and only spoken—as prescribed—for around twenty minutes. In his response Orbán revealed with total frankness that he had rehearsed the text before his trip to Austria several times aloud in preparation and shortened it where necessary so as not to exceed the length specified by the organisers. He had become a complete professional politician—in this respect too.

After lunch, we went for a walk in the beautiful court-yard of the monastery while the team of the Austrian public broadcaster ORF was preparing the best place for our interview in a projected TV documentary about Hungary. In this documentary,[4] we had shown an excerpt from his famous short speech on Heroes' Square in Budapest in June 1989 in front of a quarter of a million people. Now ten years later he proclaimed proudly in our interview: "Since then, we have built a constitutional state with firm constitutional guarantees; a market economy with good prospects; and won the respect of the democratic world. This is very important; the future of Hungary and the fifteen million Hungarians around the world depends on it." In this film, billionaire George Soros, writers Péter Esterházy and George Tabori, composer György Ligeti and conductor Georg Solti, among others, also spoke about their relationship with Hungary. It was only Orbán who mentioned the inflated figure of fifteen million Hungarians in this short statement. The first time the conservative József Antall had spoken of feeling "in his soul" as prime minister of fifteen million Hungarians was at a party meeting on 2 June 1990.

Four months after our TV interview Orbán appeared at the annual Frankfurt Book Fair because Hungary was in 1999 the guest country of the fair. I had presented the German edition of my new book—*The Hungarians: A Thousand Years of Victory in Defeat*—and thus we met accidentally at the fair. After exchanging a few words, I presented him with a signed copy and a photo was duly published in the Hungarian press.

The next time I met Orbán was after his surprising loss of the 2002 election at a political event in Vienna which I moderated on the future of the EU. While former Christian Conservative People's Party (ÖVP) vice chancellor Erhard Busek, a convinced European, argued there in favour of the rapid enlargement of the EU, Orbán tended to emphasise the primacy of national interests and noted that there was "also life outside the EU".

Our last meeting was unusual. It took place at a petrol station on 8 April 2010, three days before the parliamentary elections in Hungary, about forty miles west of Budapest.[5] During a brief conversation, Orbán told me that he was on his way to Vienna to attend an award ceremony for Wilfried Martens, the Belgian chairman of the European People's Party (EPP). The fact that he left Budapest three days before this important election shows how purposefully Orbán cultivated contacts with important Western politicians, even as opposition leader. At the same time, it was also a sign of his enormous self-confidence that he would win the elections hands down.

The impotence of the EU in conflict with an autocracy

Though I have not met him personally since then, I have followed and described his truly meteoric career in becoming the most powerful Hungarian politician of the twenty-first century. As Gideon Rachman of the *Financial Times* put it in his book *The Age of the Strongman*, the fact that Orbán was featured on the cover of the American magazine *Foreign Affairs* in September 2019 (with an extract from my Orbán biography) under the title "Autocracy Now", alongside Vladimir Putin and Xi Jinping as well as the heads of state of Turkey and the Philippines, was an astonishing degree of recognition for the head of government of a state with a population of a mere ten million.[6]

It cannot be said that the international community, and the EU Parliament in particular, ignored the measures taken by the Orbán government to establish an authoritarian system. Hungary's resolutions on state control of the media, the capture of the state apparatus, the dismantling of the rule of law, and the introduction of special taxes against foreign banks and companies, some of which were implemented in a rush after the 2010 election victory, immediately triggered sharp international criticism. The representative on freedom of the media of the Organisation for Security and Cooperation in Europe (OSCE), Dunja Mijatović, stated back in September 2010: "Laws like these are actually only known from totalitarian countries where governments restrict freedom of speech. The law does not comply with OSCE standards, which Hungary has committed to upholding."[7] In line with Orbán's frequent references to the game of football, in which attack is the best defence and one plays until victory is achieved, he has described time and again criticism from the EU as a battle in which the hard-working Hungarian people must be protected against the domestic and foreign enemies of the homeland. At the traditional national day celebration on the steps of the National Museum in Budapest on 15 March 2011, the prime minister countered his critics by arguing that Hungary was not a colony and would not allow itself to be oppressed by Brussels after the occupation by the Turks, Habsburgs and Russians.[8]

As the Fidesz government only made cosmetic changes to the controversial laws and Orbán repeatedly attacked his critics with extraordinary vigour in speeches and interviews, the EU Parliament commissioned the Portuguese Green MEP Rui Tavares to draw up a report on the state of fundamental rights in Hungary. In May 2013, a devastating 43-page document, written after a year of research, was presented to the plenary meeting of the European Parliament. Subsequently, the report was adopted with 370 votes in favour, 82 abstentions and 249 votes against. Although the European People's Party, to which Fidesz still belonged at the time, accounted for almost half of the seats, only a third of the MEPs in the European Parliament supported Hungary. The vote represented a clear political and moral defeat for the Hungarian government.

Nevertheless, the EU did not take any drastic measures against Hungary in the years that followed. Not even when, in the summer of 2014, following his second election victory, Orbán made his provocative speech in which he came out in favour of "illiberal democracy" and praised countries such as Russia, China, Turkey and Singapore as successful examples.[9]

It would take too long to list the stages on the path to Orbán's mature authoritarian state. The 2015 refugee crisis undoubtedly played a major role. From the outset, Orbán was one of the loudest voices in Europe against accepting refugees: "We don't want to see any significant minorities in our midst whose cultural background differs from ours. We want to preserve Hungary as Hungary."[10] Politically decisive was the broad-based media campaign, which was intended on the one hand to stir up fear of foreign infiltration and terrorism and on the other to assert a right to isolation by invoking national and Christian roots. The political scientist and expert on Orbán's personality László Lengyel wrote in the *European Review* in 2016: "Orbán has the feeling that Hungarian liberals and the politicians of international liberal capitalism are just as cynical hypocrites as their Christian-democratic colleagues who preach morality in order to maintain their own positions of power and cover up their raw interests [...] When he resolutely entered the European international arena in the summer of 2015, he made it clear that liberal democracy was politically weak and dysfunctional, but that in contrast to its hypocritical and mendacious model, there was the exemplary, strong, functional and outspoken model of illiberal democracy. Orbán's words are clear: the wolf should be a wolf and not pretend to be a sheep. But the sheep should not pretend to be a wolf either."[11]

As the years passed, Orbán perfected his "peacock dance" with numerous interviews in international media and on the occasion of appearances at (temporarily) friendly parties such as the German Christian Social Union (CSU) and even more so at meetings of the institutions of the European Parliament, the EU Council and the EPP. Hungary was a double beneficiary of the structure of the EU. On the one hand, the Budapest government was able to use as it wished the transfers from Brussels (around 3 per cent of GDP and 6 per cent of the budget), totalling 83 billion euros in the twenty years since entry into the union, until recently without any possibility of sanctions.[12] At the same time it was able to attack the EU in ever new variations with the accusation that it was a stooge and ally of the Hungarian-American billionaire and patron George Soros, who was portrayed as the greatest threat to the Magyars.[13] On the other hand, Hungary was long protected from the strictest possible punishment, namely the denial of voting rights under Article 7 of the EU Treaty, by the threat of veto by Poland, the member state which at that time was also being reprimanded by the EU bodies and the European courts for dismantling its independent judiciary. After the opposition's victory in the Polish parliamentary elections in October 2023, the common front with Hungary against the EU collapsed, and subsequently the EU Commission released the funds frozen as punishment against the previous government dominated by the right-wing nationalistic PiS party.

Five years after the Tavares report, on 12 September 2018, the European Parliament determined by a two-thirds majority, for the first time in the history of the EU, that a member state, namely Hungary, had seriously breached democracy, fundamental rights and the rule of law. With 448 votes in favour, 197 against and 48 abstentions, MEPs adopted the report by Dutch Green MEP Judith Sargentini. The report listed, among other things, the disappearance of the last independent TV station, the restriction of academic freedom through the expulsion of the Central European University (CEU), the misuse of EU transfers, and restrictions on the independence of the judiciary through the forced retirement of judges.

On 15 September 2022, the European Parliament denied Hungary the right to be considered a democracy by 433 votes to 123. Hungary was not a democracy and had "become a hybrid system of electoral autocracy". MEPs criticised the EU itself for not having acted decisively enough. Parliament regretted "that the lack of decisive action by the EU has contributed to the disintegration of democracy, the rule of law and fundamental rights in Hungary".[14]

Hungary is no longer considered a free democracy, but only a kind of "half" democracy. It ranks as the most corrupt EU member state, according to Transparency International, and as 72nd out of 180 countries listed on the Reporters Without Borders' index of the state of press freedom. The Fidesz party withdrew from the conservative EPP even before it was formally expelled and demonstratively cultivates close contacts with far-right and right-wing populist parties. Owing to Hungary's violations of the rule of law, the EU Commission is withholding a total of 20 billion euros in budget support and coronavirus reconstruction funds until Hungary adopts watertight rules to combat corruption and cronyism in public tenders.

After so many years of verbal admonishments, a judgment of the European Supreme Court on 14 June 2024 marked a turning point in the stormy history of Hungary's relations with the EU. The court sentenced Hungary for violations of the European laws on migrants to a fine of 200 million euros and to a daily punitive payment of one million euros, as long as the government continued to infringe the legal regulations concerning the treatment of refugees.[15]

Orbán immediately reacted with a violent attack on the judges as stooges "funded by the billionaire George Soros". And he announced in a speech on the eve of the European elections: "We must occupy Brussels, push aside their bureaucrats and take matters into our own hands." The ridiculous demagoguery failed to impress the voters at home. For the first time the ruling Fidesz party lost two of its eleven seats in the European Parliament. At the first attempt, the disappointed Fidesz insider Péter Magyar managed to win with his improvised Tisza Party almost 30 per cent of the votes and thus seven seats in the EU parliament.[16]

Putin's best man in Brussels

Particularly since the Russian invasion of Ukraine, international attention has been paid above all to Orbán's international ambitions to be recognised as Putin's preferred and most trusted ally in the EU, as his "Trojan horse", and as a European pacesetter in the transatlantic coalition of "strongmen". Already in his annual State of the Union address at the beginning of 2020, Orbán, driven by megalomaniac ambitions, declared: "We used to think that Europe was our future. Today we know: We are Europe's future!"[17]

Orbán met Putin for the first time as opposition leader in St Petersburg for a mere half-hour conversation in November 2009, five months before his election victory. Perhaps it was not only Orbán's winning streak that formed the basis for an unusual, blossoming friendship between Orbán and Putin. In his biography of Orbán, the Italian expert on Hungary Stefano Bottoni describes in detail the old rumours about alleged blackmail of the

Hungarian politician based on documents in the Russian secret service archives, but he points out that there is no documented evidence of this.[146] I myself have never found any solid evidence of these rumours.

Be that as it may, Putin and Orbán have met so far fourteen times since 2009 for friendly one-on-one talks. The Hungarian foreign minister and close confidant of the head of government, Péter Szijjártó, even received the highest Russian award for foreigners in autumn 2022 from the Russian foreign minister Sergei Lavrov, whom he warmly embraces at their frequent meetings. Although Hungary has so far supported the EU sanctions against Russia for the war against Ukraine, all media controlled by the regime represent the Russian point of view and propagate peace negotiations regardless of Ukrainian demands. Hungary also held up Finland's and Sweden's admission to NATO for a long time for no good reason. Dependence on Russian gas and oil supplies and the expansion of the Russian-built nuclear power plant on the Danube near Paks are just two elements of the close cooperation between Moscow and Budapest. There are others: the sale of residence permits to tens of thousands of Russian and Chinese citizens with the right to access the Schengen area, that is, the EU; or the veto against EU sanctions against the controversial Orthodox patriarch Cyril and against nine well-known Russian oligarchs with close ties to Putin. A symbolic proof of Orbán's closeness to Putin was the five-hour one-on-one meeting in the Kremlin three weeks before the Russian attack on Ukraine.

Hungary also maintains close relations with the authoritarian regime of Xi Jinping. In October 2023, Orbán was the only EU head of government to travel to Beijing to meet President Xi, who called him a "friend", on the sidelines of the New Silk Road summit. Here he also met Vladimir Putin, who expressly thanked Hungary for continuing to maintain relations with Russia in difficult times.[18]

On his state visit to Hungary in May 2024, as the last stop in his European tour which also took him to Paris and Belgrade, Xi said the two countries would embark on a "golden voyage" in their bilateral relations, which were "the best they have ever been". In turn, Orbán praised China as "one of the pillars of the new world order".

During the visits eighteen agreements were signed, among others for the construction of important railway links in addition to the building of the Belgrade–Budapest railway and the development of an electric car charging network in Hungary. Chinese investments worth 16.5 billion euros are currently under way in the country, estimated to account for 44 per cent of China's total direct investments in Europe.

Orbán has also established a close personal relationship with Turkish President Recep Tayyip Erdoğan, who visited Hungary twice within four months in 2023. Hungary was the only NATO country that supported

Turkey in blocking the accession of Finland and Sweden to the alliance. The firms of a Turkish multimillionaire businessman, Adnan Polat, who is close to President Erdoğan, are involved in a number of housing and solar energy projects, closely cooperating with Orbán's son-in-law, István Tiborcz, who in a few years has risen to rank eleventh on the list of the hundred richest Hungarians.

Friend of dictators, enemy of liberal democracy

It was, however, after the Russian invasion of Ukraine that the Hungarian government emerged as the embodiment of an authoritarian system providing repulsive examples of hypocrisy in its dealings with the institutions of the EU. Prime Minister Orbán has also gained international attention by blocking, delaying or watering down EU sanctions on Russia and military and financial support for Ukraine. In this sense the Hungarian government not only undermines the union's core values. Through raising obstructionism to record levels within the EU institutions, Hungary poses more and more of an unprecedented threat to the unity and functioning of the union as a whole. Thus, for example, at the time of writing, Hungary was holding up seven decisions requiring unanimity and related to Ukraine, worth 6.6 billion euros. As a senior Western European diplomat put it: "It's got to the point where nothing happens without thinking about how they could ruin it."[19]

Thus, alone in the course of 2024, Hungary blocked statements by the EU protesting against Chinese violations of human rights in Hong Kong; the adoption of a foreign agents law against domestic media assisted by donations from abroad in EU membership candidate Georgia; and the cutting off of access to eighty-one foreign media outlets (including the ORF from neutral Austria and the 444.hu news website) from Hungary. Even more scandalous was that Hungary, as the only EU state, voted against the UN resolution introducing an annual day of memory in honour of the Bosnian civilians killed in Srebrenica by Serbian troops on 11–15 July 1995.

The vote on the remembrance of the Srebrenica massacre was justified with the fake argument that it could engender hostility towards the Serbian people, although neither Serbia nor the Serbs were mentioned in the text of the UN resolution. The real reason was the mendacious role the Hungarian government has been playing in Balkan politics. On the one hand the EU commissar for neighbourhood and enlargement was a Hungarian diplomat who has been publicly accused in the EU Parliament of assisting Hungarian trouble-making in the Balkans, instead of promoting respect for European values as conditions for the projected membership of these countries in the union. On the other hand, Viktor Orbán is on close personal terms with Milorad Dodik, the rabid nationalistic president of Republika Srpska, one of the two entities of the Federation of Bosnia-

Herzegovina. The two leaders have met several times and Hungary has extended substantial loans to Republika Srpska. Orbán plays his usual double game by blaming the EU for "meddling in the internal affairs" of the area while ostentatiously supporting Dodik, who awarded him in April 2024 the highest decoration of Republika Srpska. Dodik's frequent threats of secession and merger with Serbia are seen as one of the time bombs ticking in the area. Hungary has also demanded Serbia's "immediate admission" to the EU. Serbian President Aleksandar Vučić has declined to support sanctions against Russia, is backing Dodik's provocative actions in Bosnia, and firmly refuses to recognise the Republic of Kosovo, the erstwhile Serbian province which declared its independence in 2008. Orbán's demonstrative cooperation with the two Serb politicians, who from time to time whip up dangerous nationalistic sentiments over Kosovo and Bosnia, clearly serves the strategic interests of Russia in the Balkans.

But the scope of the destructive role Hungary as member state of the EU and NATO is playing in international politics reaches far beyond this volatile region. The European Parliament condemned in a resolution of 1 June 2023 the latest ominous developments in Hungarian domestic policy and also expressed doubts about Hungary's democratic legitimacy to take over as of 1 July 2024 the rotating presidency of the EU for the next six months. This position should not be mistaken for the function of the president of the Council, elected for a period of five years by the heads of state or governments of the twenty-seven member states, or with the president of the EU Commission and the person responsible for foreign relations. The rotating presidency is largely a ceremonial one, chairing meetings and preparing the agenda of the sessions of ministers from the twenty-seven countries.

Nevertheless the EU Parliament, in a resolution adopted by 345 votes against 104 with 29 abstentions on 18 January 2024, issued a warning for the second time and called on the EU Commission "to protect the institutions, the values and the funds of the EU and to withstand blackmailing attempts". Commenting on Orbán's promises of a "constructive presidency", the critics compared it to "putting the fox in charge of the hen house".[20] Both warnings have been prescient.

On the eve of taking over the EU presidency, Orbán formed a new hard-right group called Patriots for Europe in the EU Parliament together with the leaders of the Austrian Freedom Party (FPÖ) and the Czech Yes party (ANO), Herbert Kickl and Andrej Babiš respectively. Announcing this in Vienna, together with his two partners, a jubilant Orbán predicted that the new formation "will take off like a rocket and very quickly become the largest group of the European right". The group's name is of course deceptive because these far-right populists, instead of being "for Europe", stand for the primacy of their nations and against migrants and refugees. This aside, Orbán's boast was not totally empty. With important hard-right parties quickly joining the founders, the Patriots already ranks as the third-largest group in the European Parliament.

All this was only a prelude to the unprecedented series of provocative and divisive actions undertaken by Orbán in his new position. The EU's longest-serving national leader shocked his partners by immediately embarking in his new position upon a self-dubbed "peace mission" to Kyiv, Moscow and Beijing without any of his supposed allies knowing what the point of his personal diplomacy was. Posing as a self-styled saviour, Orbán asserted that his talks with Volodymyr Zelensky, Vladimir Putin and Xi Jinping open lines of communication for a future peace deal.

Instead of the subdued international approach expected by some observers, the Hungarian presidency was used to undermine the core solidarity with Ukraine and the collective will of the EU to face up to the security threat posed by Russian aggression. He crowned his role, dubbed by *The Economist* as "the EU's pantomime villain", after attending a NATO summit in Washington, with a lightning visit to then ex-president Donald Trump, their third meeting since March 2019. Trump and Orbán paid fulsome compliments to each other. The Hungarian prime minister parroted Trump's claim that, once he was elected as president, he would "immediately put an end to the war between Russia and Ukraine".

To sum up, Viktor Orbán is not a despot, murdering or jailing opposition figures, restricting or tightly controlling exit and entry, as is done by his friends Putin and Xi. Nevertheless, he exerts practically unlimited power to make decisions in a country which is only "partly free", according to the annual report by Freedom House, the American think tank. It is a unique system in Europe, a soft autocracy, based not only on control over the judiciary, the media and the security services, but also on reliance on a small elite with a stake in the survival of complex kleptocratic financial structures. Deceit, hypocrisy and foul play have been successfully used by Orbán to construct a soft autocracy and to divide the twenty-seven-member EU from within.

For the first time, however, since 2010 a strong opposition force, the new "Tisza Party", has emerged, founded and led by a charismatic new political figure, Péter Magyar, which for the first time could pose a serious threat to Orbán's ruling Fidesz Party. The 43-year-old diplomat and lawyer was the former husband of justice minister Judit Varga. She and President Katalin Novák resigned in February 2024 after it had been revealed that Novák had granted a presidential pardon to the deputy director of a children's home involved in covering up the sexual abuse of minors. Magyar, a Fidesz insider and member of the board of several state-owned companies, immediately accused those who were really responsible for the scandal of "hiding behind the skirts of the two women". He gave up his positions, accused the Fidesz government of widespread corruption and started an opposition movement. After reviving and taking over the dormant Tisza Party, Magyar scored an unprecedented success at the elections for the European Parliament in June 2024, polling almost 30 per cent of the votes and capturing seven seats. Touring the country during the following months and exposing the sad state of the health, education and traffic systems, the brilliant speaker attracted tens of thousands of listeners. According to the polling reports published by independent research institutes at the time of this writing, the Tisza Party now has a firm lead over the Orbán party both among eligible voters and those who intend to vote in the 2026 parliamentary elections.

It remains to be seen whether the temperamental and personally somewhat unstable Péter Magyar will be able to maintain his lead and how Viktor Orbán, the hitherto absolute ruler, will respond if his political survival and his family's personal fortune are at stake.

8

GEORGE SOROS

FROM ADMIRED PHILANTHROPIST TO HATED DEMON

When rumours grow old, they become myths.

Stanisław Jerzy Lec

The two best-known, most admired and most hated Hungarians, who are also irreconcilable political enemies, are Viktor Orbán and George Soros. I have met both men several times, not to mention for interviews with ORF, the Austrian public TV channel, and described their careers and my contacts with them in my books.[1] Here I deal exclusively with the political significance of George Soros's personality and the offensive by hypocrites from Orbán to Trump against the globally active foundations he established, the Open Society Foundations. In order to understand how this offensive has developed, it is first necessary to outline Soros's personal relationship with Hungary.

Born in Budapest in 1930, Soros describes the year 1944, when he survived the Shoah, as his formative experience. Before the communist takeover, he went to London and graduated from the London School of Economics. He partly financed his studies by working as a porter and waiter. After completing his studies, he initially worked at a London merchant bank and moved to the United States in 1956. In 1970, Soros founded the Soros Fund in New York, later renamed the Quantum Fund, with $5 million in seed capital. Through currency and share speculation, the fund's assets grew to $4 billion by 1993. In 2008, Soros was the best-paid hedge fund manager in the world with an income of $1.1 billion. In its 2016 list of billionaires, *Forbes* magazine estimated his fortune at $24.9 billion, putting him in 23rd place at the time. In 2023, he fell to the 365th place on the *Forbes* list with an estimated fortune of $6.7 billion—because he had given away a total of $34 billion since 1979. In 2017, he transferred a large part of his fortune, $18 billion, to the Open Society Foundations.

I do not want to report here on his life and his successful speculations, which have been described in a number of books, but primarily on the political consequences of his activities, which began in 1979 in South Africa, as an internationally active and purposeful philanthropist, as a promoter of the "open society" in the sense of his university teacher Sir Karl Popper.[2]

The role of the Soros foundations

There are several reasons why one can speak of his foundations as a unique phenomenon. George Soros was by far the most important individual donor in the countries of the former Soviet sphere of influence. Never before had such a wealthy man been prepared to give away the majority of his fortune specifically to promote an open society, to defend the values of liberal democracy and the rights of minorities. He did not strive for fame but for peaceful change in Eastern Europe, and through the dual dynamics of political upheaval and his increasingly extensive philanthropic activities, he himself became an architect of change.

When I conducted a long television interview with him in 1995, he already enjoyed an international reputation as a "one-man Marshall Plan" (in the words of *Newsweek*), as the most influential foreigner in the entire former Soviet empire. Strobe Talbott, then US deputy secretary of state, said in an interview with the *New Yorker* about his role: "We are working with him as we would with a friendly, allied, independent entity, if not a government. We are trying to coordinate our position on the ex-communist states with Germany, France, Britain—and George Soros."[3]

All this happened on the political stage of Eastern Europe in the form of a series of improvisations. Soros did not even have an archive of his donations until 1994.

As far as the dimensions of the individual projects are concerned, only three examples should be mentioned here. In the midst of the chaos following the collapse of the Soviet Union, 30,000 Russian scientists received around $100 million; $250 million was spent on an ambitious programme to publish revised Russian text-books and train Russian teachers; around the same time, Soros spent $50 million helping the people of Sarajevo, the Bosnian capital besieged by Serb forces, to restore gas, electricity and water supplies.

Despite the worldwide activities of the foundations in thirty-five countries, the political and cultural conse-quences for the undermining of dictatorship were per-haps nowhere as significant as in the home country of the philanthropist, who has since become a US citizen. Soros had already established his first foundation here in 1984, that is, still under the conditions of the weakened Kádár regime, and founded the Central European University in 1991.

It is precisely because of the international smear cam-paign against George Soros, which began in Hungary in 2015, that it is particularly important to cite an inde-pendent and critical historian of Hungary such as Stefano Bottoni. In his book on Viktor Orbán, the Italian academic, who was a leading member of staff at the Historical Institute of the Hungarian Academy of Sciences between 2000 and 2019, stated: "No one has played such an important role in the development and material support of Fidesz and Viktor Orbán as George Soros. Through his foundation, he had a significant influence on the Hungarian system change and the democratic institutions after 1989."[4]

The donation of 500 modern photocopiers and electronic equipment worth $4 million to libraries, hospitals and not least Fidesz and other civil society groups has enabled the freer flow of information despite the control of the weakened state party. Many activists and, later, leading politicians of the Fidesz party, founded in March 1988, received one-year scholarships to universities in Britain or the United States. Bottoni also mentions that Orbán himself lived largely from the support of the Soros Foundation from April 1988 until the 1990 elections: first with a "very decent salary" at a Central European research centre and from September 1989 with a nine-month, $10,000 Soros scholarship as a guest of Pembroke College in Oxford. He returned to Budapest after four months because of the first free elections in Hungary.

A third of the members of the Hungarian parliament elected in 1990 received scholarships or material support from the Soros Foundation. A total of 3,200 young Hungarians (politicians, writers, translators, students) enjoyed scholarships from the foundation to study at foreign universities. According to the foundation, aid to Hungary since 1984 has totalled over $400 million.

But even this achievement is dwarfed by the international significance of the Central European University

(CEU). Since its foundation in 1991–1992, 18,000 students from 130 countries have graduated from CEU. It is recognised as one of the world's best universities in the fields of politics, international studies and philosophy. Soros has secured the future of this unique institution in the long term with donations totalling $2 billion, despite its forced exodus to Vienna in 2019–2020.[5]

The Hungarian communications expert Mária Vásárhelyi rightly noted on the occasion of George Soros's ninetieth birthday that since Count Stephan Széchenyi (1791–1860), no one has donated as much from their own fortune to science in Hungary as Soros, the Hungarian Jew and US citizen.[6] The rector of CEU between 2016 and 2021, the Canadian contemporary historian Michael Ignatieff, said something similar in an interview: "No one has done as much for Hungary as he, and no one has been so unjustly vilified."[7]

The anti-Soros campaign

So how and why did the admired philanthropist George Soros first become the head of a global conspiracy to undermine his own nation in Hungary and then the epitome of worldwide evil? In the first place he became the target of a propaganda campaign in his home country that was unique in Hungarian history and utilised all technical means. It was a US campaign and communications consultant, Arthur Finkelstein, who, together with his assistant George Birnbaum, had the "brilliant idea" of turning billionaire George Soros into a "monster", the new enemy of Hungary. Finkelstein and Birnbaum had worked for Benjamin Netanyahu, the Israeli politician, who recommended them to Viktor Orbán, then leader of the opposition, before the 2010 election campaign.

Based on an interview with George Birnbaum, the Swiss journalist Hannes Grassegger reported on the success of the "Finkelstein formula" in Hungary in a major report in *Das Magazin* at the beginning of 2019.[8] This formula demanded that every successful campaign needs an opponent. Finkelstein had found his ideal opponent in Soros. "The perfect opponent is one you hit again and again and who never hits back," explained Birnbaum in the interview. Soros was the figure who perfectly epitomised big business conspiring against little Hungary. What's more, he was born in Hungary, so he was not unknown.

Birnbaum was still raving about him years later: "It was so obvious. It was the simplest of all products. You just had to package and market it." The "Soros monster" was born, a Jewish multi-billionaire with a global network against whom the entire nation had to unite behind Viktor Orbán in order to defeat him, just as it had against the Ottomans, the Habsburgs and, in 1956, the Soviets and communists. Birnbaum said that Finkelstein enjoyed "enormous trust" from Orbán. The Hungarian leader's closest political advisor, the enigmatic Árpád Habony,[9] who hardly ever appears in public, even founded a joint consultancy firm with Finkelstein in London. Finkelstein died in August 2017; Hungary was his last and probably most successful project.

In his report, the Swiss author points out an "aspect that is as important as it is strange": "Two Jewish political advisors make a Jew the target of a campaign with anti-Semitic overtones." Finkelstein and Birnbaum had resorted to one of the oldest anti-Semitic subjects in the West: that of the avaricious Jew who seeks to dominate the world. "When we planned the campaign, we didn't think for a second that Soros was Jewish," said Birnbaum while trying to refute the accusations in a barely credible statement.

Even though Orbán never used the word "Jew" in the campaign against Soros, which formally began against his ideas about refugees in autumn 2015, it has always had an anti-Semitic connotation. In 2018, for example, Orbán said that they were fighting against an "opponent" who was "different" and had "no homeland of his own", who "feels that the whole world belongs to him".[10] The year before, the Budapest government had put up huge posters under the slogan "Stop Brussels", showing a close-up of a grinning Soros: "Let's not let Soros have the last laugh." Other posters showed him as a puppeteer making the opposition politicians dance. No wonder that in a country where two-thirds of the Jews perished in the Holocaust, yellow Stars of David were often added to the barely concealed message of these Soros posters.

Orbán, who had already effortlessly transformed himself from a liberal left-of-centre politician in 1994 into an eloquent nationalist, proved to be a brilliant student of Finkelstein and a virtuoso of hypocrisy. With this unprecedented mobilisation against the Soros foundations as a "background power", George Soros was built up into the symbol of an existential threat to Hungary. In his speeches and weekly radio interviews, Orbán himself repeatedly set the tone of the campaign against the alleged plan to flood Hungary and Europe with migrants, to turn Hungary into a country of immigration, and to rob the country and the continent of its cultural identity. When the EU Commission finally opened proceedings against Hungary for violating the elementary foundations of the rule of law, he declared in the Hungarian parliament: "The Brussels bureaucrats are working on the implementation of the Soros plan and are eating out of Soros's hand."[11]

The global attacks against Soros

Viktor Orbán is proud of his internationally successful feat of hypocrisy, transforming a once admired benefactor of Hungary into a villain hated by autocrats and their partisans worldwide. At the 2023 Budapest conference of the right-wing US Conservative Political Action Conference, he boasted that Hungary owed to Soros the global success of Orbán's policy against the ideology of the open society: "We ended up on the front pages of the world press because we took up the fight against Soros's migrant programme and against the ideology of the open society advocated by the NGOs and defended our homeland."[12]

The plan invented by Finkelstein and Birnbaum and implemented by Orbán and his government apparatus to demonise a rich philanthropist as a rootless financier with political ambitions has indeed achieved worldwide success. The autocrats and right-wing movements that want to stage pseudo-election campaigns today can simply draw upon the diverse, freely available and adaptable anti-Soros conspiracy theories from the web.

The Open Society Foundations financially support civil society NGOs in the areas of education and minority rights, media freedom and anti-corruption initiatives. Vladimir Putin forced the Soros foundations to leave Russia back in 2015 because they were funding human rights organisations such as Memorial, which was conducting investigations into Soviet terror.[13]

Other autocrats followed suit. In 2018, Turkish President Recep Tayyip Erdoğan accused liberal human rights activist Osman Kavala, who has since been sentenced to life imprisonment, of being part of a Soros-led conspiracy against the Turkish state: "Who is behind him? The famous Hungarian Jew George Soros. This is a man who has the task of dividing and shattering nations."[14] Five years later, Orbán celebrated the election success of his "old friend" Erdoğan as the salvation of Europe and a victory against a candidate "supported by Soros".

As the Soros foundations have also supported Palestinian rights groups and liberal institutions in Israel, Yair Netanyahu, son of the Israeli prime minister and friend of the Orbán regime, insulted Soros on Facebook and circulated a cartoon showing him dangling the globe in front of a reptilian creature.

In recent years, the campaign against Soros has also intensified in the United States. At the end of October 2018, Soros received a letter bomb from a Trump supporter. He was accused by President Trump of financing illegal migration to the United States. Trump supporters accused him of being involved in the "stolen" 2020 elections. In the race for the presidential candidacy for 2024, Trump repeatedly used anti-Semitic stereotypes. In mid-July 2023, his campaign team sent an email to his supporters: a picture shows Soros pulling Joe Biden's strings as a puppeteer. Trump also made accusations against Soros in connection with his indictment for allegedly paying hush money to a porn actress in New York in spring 2023: the district attorney, he said, was "hand-picked and financed by George Soros".[15]

Elon Musk, the richest man in the world, with a fortune of around $250 billion, attacked Soros personally in May 2023: "Soros hates humanity." The verbal attacks on Twitter (X) came after Soros's fund management sold all shares in the Tesla car factory run by Musk.[16] Soros also became the target of savage attacks in India after he sharply criticised Prime Minister Narendra Modi's Hindu nationalist course in a speech at the 2023 Munich Security Conference.

It would take too long to list all the accusations made on various occasions by right-wing candidates and movements in Poland and Slovakia, Bulgaria and Romania, Brazil and Malaysia, against Soros and the human rights organisations he directly or indirectly supports. The most visible and significant international consequence of the application of the "Finkelstein–Orbán formula" is the invention of Soros as the perfect villain. The comparison of Soros to the character Emmanuel Goldstein in George Orwell's novel *1984* is obvious. He is also seen as "a hidden power behind every scandal and every conspiracy against the common people".[17]

George Soros, who turned 94 on 12 August 2024, transferred the leadership of the Open Society Foundations to his son Alexander, born in 1985, in June 2023. He has announced a controversial shift of priorities in favour of supporting the Democrats in the United States and cutting the staff and budget of the foundations in Europe. In the foreseeable future, however, this will hardly change the Soros phobia in the world of autocrats and certainly not the anti-Soros campaign as a major factor in the Orbán regime's foreign and domestic policy. Thus in June 2024 Orbán still viciously attacked the judges of the EU's supreme court as "Soros's puppets" for sentencing Hungary to a fine of 200 million euros for violations of legal rules concerning migrants and the use of EU funds.

After fifteen years in power, all Fidesz politicians and the friendly Hungarian oligarchs who have become so filthy rich kowtow towards Viktor Orbán. Internationally, too, the political wind is blowing from a different direction from that of the 1990s, when the activities of the Soros foundations were at their ideological and financial peak. Once the pacesetter of democratic reforms, Hungary has now become the most corrupt and Putin-friendly member state in the EU thanks to the Orbán clique.[18] If you read Orbán's speeches, which are always garnished with Soros attacks, you can't help thinking of the archbishop in the great Austrian writer Thomas Bernhard's novel *Extinction*. As a literary critic put it, the figure from the Vatican, who has been romantically linked to the protagonist's mother for decades, "pretends to be such a prince of the church that he not only repels, but also fascinates because of the virtuoso effort of his mendacity".[19] This is roughly how one could also describe the hypocrisy of the autocrat in Buda Castle, who is so dangerous for the future of liberal democracy in Europe and so successful in maintaining his power; a perfect turncoat, who of all people has levelled innumerable accusations of hypocrisy against the philanthropist who was once his personal benefactor.

And the fate of George Soros? Is he, with his liberal worldview, ultimately the loser in the international battle of ideas? Will fake historians in the service of dictators succeed in depicting him as the perfect villain? I believe that his true legacy will not be the billions he gave the Open Society Foundations from his personal fortune, but the ideas he has so passionately defended throughout his life. The battle between liberal democracy and authoritarian temptation, in Europe as well as in the United States, is still continuing. That is why the final judgement on George Soros's legacy must remain open.

9

SEBASTIAN KURZ

THE MAN BEHIND THE MASKS

Some people lack the gift of seeing the truth. But what honesty their lies breathe!

Stanisław Jerzy Lec

In autumn 2023, three unusual films were presented about the former Austrian chancellor Sebastian Kurz, who had announced his complete retirement from politics less than two years earlier, on 2 December 2021. The three film documentaries, which were premiered in quick succession, could also be given the collective title "A Star Is Born" albeit they are different in character.

There have been resignations of top Austrian politicians, but never before have three films been presented about a former chancellor, simultaneously and so soon after his departure. "I am neither a saint nor a criminal," Kurz said in his resignation speech. He spoke of a witch-hunt against his person through insinuations and suspicions. The Central Prosecution Office for Corruption and Economy had accused him of perjury in a hearing before a parliamentary inquiry, and on 23 February 2024 he received an eight-month suspended sentence in a court in Vienna. This conviction was overturned in May 2025. At the time of writing, no indictment had yet been issued about Kurz's alleged involvement in commissioning and financing fake opinion polls. As the rise and fall of Sebastian Kurz was described in detail in my previous book, *Austria Behind the Mask* (2023), the background to the charges will not be dealt with here.[1] Kurz denies any wrongdoing.

Three films about Sebastian Kurz

Even before the films were completed, it was clear that Sebastian Kurz, who always emphasised his innocence, would sooner or later be put on trial. So why three costly film portrayals with Kurz in the leading role? It had long been known that the author and director Kurt Langbein was preparing a critical documentary entitled *Projekt Ballhausplatz* and subtitled (in English translation) "The Rise and Fall of Sebastian Kurz". However, only one week before the release of the Langbein film, the director Sascha Köllnreitner, previously known only for sports and advertising films, out of the blue also presented a documentary of Kurz's career with the title *Kurz: Der Film*. Both films were released in Austrian cinemas almost simultaneously. At the same time, it became known that the Croatian director Jakov Sedlar had also completed a one-hour film in English about Kurz entitled *Sebastian Kurz: The Truth*. I watched all three films and also read numerous interviews with the directors and some of the people who spoke about Kurz in the films.

The film *Projekt Ballhausplatz*, produced by Kurt Langbein, a reputable independent director, is a well-made compilation of mostly critical interviews and excerpts from ORF videos about the accusations against Kurz and his defence. Neither Kurz himself nor key ÖVP (Austrian People's Party) politicians were prepared to grant interviews. As a result of this boycott, the elements of tension are missing and the overall result is likely to give the impression, at any rate in the eyes of his supporters, of bias against Kurz.

While the details of the financing for the Langbein film have been published, the sources of funding for the other two films are unknown. Kurt Langbein, probably the most well-informed expert on Kurz after reviewing thousands of hours of ORF archive material with and about Kurz, has analysed the forms and substance of the ex-chancellor's virtuoso use of hypocrisy in an extensive interview. He was particularly impressed by his versatility: "none of it was real, Kurz always wore a mask [...] When he speaks, his statements almost always seem plausible, even if you know that what he says is not true."[2] The director found it particularly dramatic that Kurz and a dozen people had been able to take over the People's Party and then the entire republic, losing power ultimately only because of the release of the "Ibiza video" in which his ally, Heinz-Christian Strache: the far-right FPÖ Vice-Chancellor was secretly filmed offering public contracts to a woman posing as a Russian oligarch's niece.[3]

The image of the ex-chancellor shown in *Kurz: Der Film* was quite different and was well received at the festive presentation attended by numerous former and current ÖVP grandees. The political scientist Peter Filzmaier found little new in the film: "Several photos and sequences even looked as if they had been shot and provided by the Kurz team."[4] In the film, Kurz is presented on the global political stage, especially as a widely admired counterpart of Angela Merkel in respect of his migration policy. Key members of the Kurz team appear and explain the reasons why they have been so successful. Former chancellor Wolfgang Schüssel of the ÖVP justifies the coalition with the Freedom Party, and the defeated presidential candidate (in 2016), former president of Parliament Andreas Kohl, praises Kurz to the skies. It was probably no coincidence that Kurz explicitly thanked only these two ÖVP leaders by name for their advice in his farewell speech.

However, director Köllnreitner has not produced a pure propaganda piece. He also allows some critics to have their say, albeit without harsh statements, which have been skilfully abridged. Although the photos of Kurz in cosy harmony with President Vladimir Putin of Russia or Viktor Orbán of Hungary are not shown, we see for a few moments a highly symbolic book that Kurz was supposedly reading while travelling: the English edition of a work by a high-ranking politician of the Orbán government on the basic policy of the ruling Fidesz party.[5]

The most fitting analysis of this Kurz-friendly film comes from the authoritative media expert Fritz Hausjell, whose critical interview was not included in the film "for dramaturgical reasons". According to him, the classic recipe for such products in favour of a client is one-third criticism, two-thirds positive arguments. In this film, however, the ratio is 1:4 to 1:6, depending on the topic. And, Hausjell continues: "The beneficiary is clear: Kurz and his team. The purpose too: reputation management ahead of court proceedings and a possible political re-entry into politics."[6]

Personally, I found the film by Croatian director Jakov Sedlar, *Sebastian Kurz: The Truth*, for several reasons more revealing than the pro-Kurz documentary previously described. This one-hour film cannot be seen in cinemas, but can be rented for 24 hours on the streaming platform Vimeo for a fee of 9.99 euros. It was made in English, with German subtitles. The text is spoken by 74-year-old US actor Armand Assante. Only Kurz himself and the only Austrian interviewee, former ÖVP secretary general and agriculture minister

Elisabeth Köstinger, speak German (and are subtitled in English).

The Croatian director is no unknown quantity. Sedlar, born in 1952, has made nationalistic films about the Jasenovac concentration camp in Croatia during the Nazi era and the dubious Croatian president Franjo Tudjman (1922–1999). His documentary *Jasenovac: The Truth*, about the concentration camp in which 83,000 Jews, Serbs, Roma and Croatian opponents of the fascist Ustasha regime were murdered, sparked outrage. Sedlar trivialised the terror, reduced the number of victims to 20,000–30,000, and focused on communist oppression. Academics, victims' associations and the Jewish community protested. The historian, publicist and Holocaust survivor Slavko Goldstein condemned the film as "a collection of half-truths, falsifications and lies".[175]

That a filmmaker with such a background was contacted by the Kurz team and (according to Sedlar in his interviews with Croatian newspapers) received material from Kurz himself is characteristic. It is also remarkable that his contacts with Israel and the fight against anti-Semitism are focused on in the documentary. Commendatory Jewish voices are quoted at length about Kurz: David Harris, the long-time ex-president of the American Jewish Committee, the New York rabbi Arthur Schneier, the initiator of the Vienna Shoah Wall of Names Kurt Yakov Tutter, and Israel's prime minister

Benjamin Netanyahu. On the occasion of Kurz's speech to commemorate the 80th anniversary of the Anschluss at the annual conference of the American Jewish Committee in Jerusalem, he is almost canonised by David Harris: "Kurz had made history with this speech." That Federal Chancellor Franz Vranitzky and Federal President Thomas Klestil had already settled accounts with the victim myth in a moving way before the Knesset in 1993 and 1994 respectively is ignored in the film. Nothing is said about the proximity of Kurz and his Freedom Party (FPÖ) government partners to the autocrats in Moscow and Budapest.

Overall it must be stressed that not a single critical word is uttered in the 62 minutes of the film about the former chancellor or his actions. Throughout the film, Kurz is only referred to by his first name. Apart from the sequence of still images and image videos of Kurz with Angela Merkel, whom he outshone with his "closing of the Balkan route", as well as with countless heads of state and government, the former US ambassador to Austria Trevor Traina, who was sent by Trump to Vienna, appears as an enthusiastic fan: "Sebastian" has made Austria relevant again in the United States after Kreisky and has managed to bring Austria onto the world political stage. Kurz also appears in numerous shots with children and young people, with disabled people and pensioners, mixed with proud monologues about the achievements of his term of office.

All of this, together with the interspersed hymns of praise from former cabinet minister Elisabeth Köstinger, seems as exaggerated as a bad advertising film: the child prodigy "Sebastian" could walk at the age of ten months and spoke in full sentences at the age of one. The parody-like formulations are of course not surprising: they come from the author Judith Grohmann. According to *Der Spiegel*, the whole of Austria mocked the "official biography" of Kurz she wrote in 2019. It reads in parts like "a mixture of fan book and kitsch novel, here and there also like a genuflection, a homage and a declaration of love".[7]

In the film, Judith Grohmann also describes Kurz as "confident", "authentic", "determined", "objective and polite"; he has "a great talent for listening to people", is "respectful, always friendly", "down to earth", "very close to nature", "an embodiment of Austrian charisma" and "a formative figure in the new politics of the twenty-first century".

All of this confirms the apt observation by Viennese philosopher Isolde Charim about the qualities attributed to Kurz in the ÖVP: "Kurz is our star, you can hear, an outstanding, an extraordinary, an exceptional, even a talent of the century. From the outside, it seems like a mutually reinforcing, collective hysteria [...] His special talent lies in creating the belief that he is such an exceptional talent."[8]

This film was probably made primarily to support Sebastian Kurz's international reputation as an entrepreneur and his possible return to politics, such as a top position in Brussels (according to former ambassador Trevor Traina), which is discreetly hinted at at the end. There is not a single critical word about this "politically gifted actor with a switched-off internal moral warning system", as the liberal writer Armin Thurnher put it.[9] The two pro-Kurz films are silent about the takeover of key positions (including the foreign, interior and defence ministries) by the Freedom Party in the ÖVP–FPÖ coalition under Kurz as chancellor. The catastrophic consequences of this for the reputation of Austria, which have been described in numerous articles in the world press, do not exist in this illusory world built on his fictitious charisma.

It is worth quoting Kurz's justification from a book of interviews with a columnist of the mass-circulation daily *Kronen Zeitung*: "I won't say anything bad about Heinz-Christian Strache [former vice chancellor] and the FPÖ government team [...] We worked well together over a certain period of time. I am very proud of what has been achieved during this time and in this government. And Heinz-Christian Strache can be too."[10] In his passionate study of Kurz's two chancellorships, Armin Thurnher prophetically states: "He continues his career in the political-lobbyist part of finance capital unperturbed, and nowadays that means his political career has only just begun. He is and remains, to paraphrase [the nineteenth-century dramatist Johann] Nestroy, an investor in himself."[11]

The business career of Sebastian Kurz

After stepping down as federal chancellor, Kurz began his business career in 2022 as a "global strategist" with German-American billionaire Peter Thiel. Kurz had already got to know him during his time as foreign minister at the Munich Security Conference. Kurz's impeccable political presentation skills, his way of being "incredibly communicative and attentive", and "the stylised, embellished, controlled face"[12] must have impressed the investor with his bizarre theories even back then. When it was announced in August 2021 that Thiel was to receive a prize in memory of Frank Schirrmacher, a respected German political writer, he proposed that Kurz give the laudatory speech. Owing to the political turmoil in Vienna, Kurz was unable to fulfil this wish. The communiqué itself sparked ridicule and outrage on social media: "Peter Thiel as Schirrmacher Prize winner, Kurz as laudator? Schirrmacher is spinning in his grave," wrote journalist Nils Minkmar, for example. Meanwhile literary scholar Johannes Franzen criticised Thiel on Deutsche Welle.

Born in 1967, Thiel has a fortune of \$7.8 billion thanks to successful investments in the technology sector with his hedge fund, according to Bloomberg. It is his involvement on the right-wing fringes of American politics, as a Trump supporter and promoter of extreme right-wing Republican candidates in the congressional elections as well as ultra-right organisations, that explains his poor international reputation.[13]

Thiel has made no secret of his view of the world in his books, articles and statements. He goes much further than most libertarians, as the supporters of extreme individualism are known in the United States. The *Neue Zürcher Zeitung* describes him as follows: "He considers democracy and freedom to be incompatible, and he also thinks little of economic competition. This is something for losers. The goal of every entrepreneur must be to achieve a monopoly position, as only then can he fully realise his goals. In his opinion, the efficient management of states should be modelled on the management of corporations. Elections and parliamentary procedures are only a brake on this. He even expressed scepticism about women's voting rights because they generally pursue a social rather than libertarian agenda and thus prevent economic growth."[14]

Thiel not only supported Trump's 2016 election campaign with $1.2 million. In 2022, he donated $10 million each to the campaigns of two leading employees of his hedge fund, Blake Masters and J. D. Vance, who wanted to become senators in the states of Arizona and Ohio respectively. Only Vance managed to win—also thanks to the help of Donald Trump, and in 2025 he became US vice president.

It is not known, and Sebastian Kurz does not talk about, what he is actually doing for the financial interests of his new boss's investment companies. In any case, he praises Thiel beyond measure, saying he is "an exceptional figure and has managed to become one of the most successful investors in the world. Thiel has a feeling like no other for where the world is heading, how trends are changing our lives and which innovations will prevail. I have always appreciated the exchange with him and have always benefited from this exchange during my time in politics [...] I like people with clear convictions, perhaps that is what connects us."[15]

Officially, we know only that the former chancellor has forged contracts and provided analyses for Thiel—a job he has since given up. His own company is a consulting firm that specialises in geopolitical and business appraisals as well as assistance in the search for investors. He specialises in the Middle East and is opening another office in Dubai.[16]

Kurz opened an office in Tel Aviv with a high-profile Israeli. Shalev Hulio, who also appears briefly in Jakov Sedlar's film, is the founder and former head of the Israeli NSO Group, which specialises mainly in surveillance technology and developed the controversial Pegasus spyware, among other things. Its customers for spyware included Azerbaijan, Saudi Arabia, the United Arab Emirates, Hungary, Poland and Spain. Here we cannot deal with the report of the EU Parliament's committee of inquiry into the so-called Pegasus scandal. However, that an Austrian ex-chancellor should found a joint cyber-security company, called "Dream", to protect critical infrastructure with the former head of the Pegasus manufacturer in October 2022 naturally triggered international media coverage.[17] That Kurz's business is flourishing in the Middle East is probably related to the fact that, according to business people based there, he is "incredibly well connected with the highest decision-makers" in the Arab world.[18]

Soon after Kurz's departure from politics due to corruption investigations, part of the Kurz team moved from the Federal Chancellery and the ÖVP headquarters to a shared office address with Kurz. In the very first year, his SK Management GmbH generated a profit of 1.9 million euros.[19] Since then not only has his annual profit doubled to 3.9 million euros, but Kurz became in two years, at any rate on paper, a multimillionaire. The company "Dream", in which he has a 15 per cent holding, is now valued at 1.1 billion dollars. It operates three firms in Tel Aviv, Abu Dhabi and Vienna and currently employs 150 people.[20]

Can there be a political comeback?

The presence of entrepreneur Sebastian Kurz with his well-calculated appearances remains an unpredictable factor in Austrian domestic and foreign policy—regardless of possible future trials. That Kurz has attacked the German government and in particular the Foreign

Ministry with conspicuous vigour, in an interview with the mass-circulation newspaper *Bild* during the refugee debate, seems strange for an entrepreneur who is supposedly no longer politically active. It seems even stranger that he is backing the controversial Tesla boss Elon Musk. The multi-billionaire and friend of Thiel had criticised German NGOs, which, according to him, use taxpayers' money to bring illegal migrants from the coast of Africa to Italy. Kurz also attacked the EU and complained that "the smugglers decide who comes to us— not the sovereign states or the EU".[21]

At the same time, Kurz has not uttered a single critical word about Viktor Orbán, even though the Hungarian head of government ordered the release of almost 2,000 people smugglers in prison. On the contrary, he appears almost demonstratively at events in Hungary: for example, he had himself photographed shaking hands warmly with Orbán in front of the Austrian and Hungarian flags at Orbán's official residence in the Carmelite Monastery in Budapest. The pictures and the official Hungarian announcement about the meeting, which centred on bilateral relations, Christian values and the EU elections, gave the impression of an Austro-Hungarian summit meeting.

When asked by *Der Standard*, his office said that Kurz had not influenced the visual presentation, nor had he consulted with the Austrian government or been commissioned to talk to Orbán by business partners.

Hungary had merely invited Kurz to the World Athletics Championships "as a private individual", especially as he is in regular contact with Orbán, the report continues. Political issues were "naturally" discussed anyway. And what does the Foreign Ministry say? "As a private person, Sebastian Kurz can meet whomever he wants."[22] This is a classic example of hypocrisy, not only on the part of the star actor but also, in a supporting role, on the part of the government apparatus.

An early biography of Kurz by a German journalist, Paul Ronzheimer, stated: "Kurz had already built up a close relationship with him [Orbán] by this time [as foreign minister in 2015]; they talk a lot on the phone and get on well."[23] This close relationship with Orbán is probably also the explanation for Kurz's good relations as federal chancellor with Orbán's high-ranking friends, the right-wing populist Slovenian prime minister Janez Janša (who has since been voted out of office) and the authoritarian Serbian president Aleksandar Vučić. During his time in office, Kurz also met the Russian president (four times in 2018!) and sealed Austria's almost total dependence on Russian gas (until 2040).

Even before the Ibiza bomb burst, the well-meaning German biographer found the closeness of Kurz's government team to Russia "worrying". "Kurz already as foreign minister was on excellent terms with Russian foreign minister Sergei Lavrov, he had also brought people into his cabinet who have great sympathy for Putin's strongman principle and want to push for an improvement in Austria's relations with Russia."[24]

So is Sebastian Kurz really just acting as a private individual when he vehemently attacks the German government in the largest German-language tabloid and demonstratively cultivates friendship with Putin's Hungarian friend Viktor Orbán? Isn't he rather pretending to be a private person, while in reality he is perfecting the new role of shadow chancellor? The international "child prodigy", as the world's youngest foreign minister and youngest head of government, has become the youngest shadow chancellor, who can determine the political fate of his successor as he sees fit.

Karel Schwarzenberg, former Czech foreign minister (2007–2009, 2010–2013), the incorruptibly sharp critic of the political elite of the Austrian Second Republic, summarised the Kurz era in gloomy words: "Unfortunately, I got the impression very early on that Kurz is a complete fake. He has [...] pursued a ruthlessly selfish policy that has led to his downfall. This period was a catastrophe for Austria [...] I said even then: if Sebastian Kurz ends up as I expect, it could also be the end of the ÖVP."[25]

Schwarzenberg could be right. In the long decades of reporting and studying contemporary history, however, I have never seen or experienced anyone who, changing roles from situation to situation, in the courtroom or in the chancery, has been so immaculate and so untouchable, so controlled and so changeable, preserving his outward appearance and excelling with memorised words, such a virtuoso of political hypocrisy in the role of victim as well as that of accuser, as the 38-year-old "political pensioner with a return ticket", Sebastian Kurz.

NOTES

PREFACE

1. Reinhard Bingener and Markus Wehner, *Die Moskau-Connection: Das Schröder-Netzwerk und Deutschlands Weg in die Abhängigkeit*, Munich, 2023, p. 270.
2. Quoted from Jean Starobinski, *Montaigne: Denken und Existenz*, Munich, 1986, p. 14.
3. Friedrich Nietzsche, *Götzen-Dämmerung*, quoted in Starobinski, *Montaigne*, p. 459.
4. Norbert Mappes-Niediek, *Krieg in Europa: Der Zerfall Jugoslawiens und der überforderte Kontinent*, Berlin, 2022, p. 358.
5. Starobinski, *Montaigne*, p. 15.
6. Thomas Bernhard, *Heldenplatz*, Frankfurt am Main, 1988, p. 112.
7. Montaigne, quoted in Starobinski, *Montaigne*, p. 13.

1. VIOLENCE AND RESISTANCE: ENCOUNTERS WITH ACTORS OF RUSSIAN POLITICS

1. For details, see Masha Gessen, *Der Mann ohne Gesicht*, Munich, 2012, pp. 167–183; Karen Dawisha, *Putin's Kleptocracy*, New York, 2014, pp. 104–223; Catherine Belton, *Putins Netz*, Hamburg, 2022, pp. 110–147.

2. The official cause of death was a heart attack. As the autopsy found no traces of this, Narusova arranged for a second autopsy, the results of which she kept "outside Russia as life insurance" for herself "in a safe country". BBC News, 5 March 2018.

3. *Novaya Gazeta Europe*, 18 April 2023. Although Narusova denied that she enjoys an exceptional position thanks to Putin's protection, the 72-year-old university professor's political future depends on him.

4. Belton, *Putins Netz*, pp. 145–146.

5. Quoted from Anna Politkovskaya, *Csakis a tiszta igazat*, Budapest, 2022, p. 450.

6. As recently as 28 August 2015, former Duma deputy Mikhail Glushchenko was sentenced to seventeen years in prison for masterminding the murder of Galina Starovoitova. TASS, 28 August 2015.

7. Vladimir Kara-Murza, opposition politician, journalist and historian, was sentenced to twenty-five years in prison on 17 April 2023 for high treason.

8. ARD interview with Boris Nemtsov on 10 December 2014, https://www.youtube.com/watch?v=Sh1Cap-IWrU.

9. A BBC team reported in a documentary on 28 March 2022 on a named intelligence officer as a possible mastermind.

10. Quoted in Christian Buckard, *Arthur Koestler: Ein extremes Leben*, Munich, 2004, p. 166.

11. See Paul Lendvai, *Auf schwarzen Listen: Erlebnisse eines Mitteleuropäers*, new edition, Vienna, 2004, pp. 293–299.

12. Paul Lendvai, *Der Ungarn-Aufstand 1956: Eine Revolution und ihre Folgen*, Munich, 2006.

2. THE SOVIET UNION: THE MARCH THROUGH DISILLUSIONMENT

1. Quoted in Andreas Rödder, *Eine kurze Geschichte der Gegenwart*, Munich, 2016, p. 11.
2. Paul Hollander, *Political Pilgrims: Western Intellectuals in Search of the Good Society*, 4th edition, London, 1997. Hollander fled Hungary in 1956, studied in London and Princeton, and was a professor of sociology at the University of Massachusetts Amherst.
3. Paul Hollander, *Political Pilgrims*, p. xlvii.
4. Anne Hartmann, *"I came, I saw, I will write": Lion Feuchtwanger in Moscow 1937: A Documentation*, Göttingen, 2017.
5. Emil Ludwig, "Unterredung mit Stalin", in *Neue Freie Presse* (Vienna), 2–4 June 1932.
6. Emil Ludwig, *Nine Etched from Life*, New York, 1934, pp. 346–348 (in German: *Führer Europas*, Amsterdam, 1934).
7. Paul Hollander, *Political Pilgrims*, p. 171.
8. Joseph E. Davies, *Als USA-Botschafter in Moskau*, Zurich, 1943, p. 217 (in English: *Mission to Moscow*, New York, 1941).
9. Sidney and Beatrice Webb, *Soviet Communism*, New York, 1936, p. 804.
10. Paul Hollander, *Political Pilgrims*, p. xlix. For the controversies surrounding the posthumous withdrawal of the Pulitzer Prize, see S. J. Taylor, *Stalin's Apologist*, New York, 1990.
11. Statement by the Pulitzer Prize jury, 21 November 2003; National Public Radio, 8 May 2022.

12. Hans Magnus Enzensberger, *Tumult*, Berlin, 2014, p. 32, quoted on Deutschlandfunk, 9 November 2014.

13. *Taz*, 10 March 2000. The original letter from Moscow to Unseld was shown in an exhibition about Enzensberger at the Berlin Literaturhaus.

14. Kai Diekmann, *Ich war BILD: Ein Leben zwischen Schlagzeilen, Staatsaffären und Skandalen*, Munich, 2023.

15. Walter Laqueur, *Mythos der Revolution: Deutungen und Fehldeutungen der Sowjetgeschichte*, Frankfurt am Main, 1967 (in English: *The Fate of the Revolution: Interpretations of Soviet History*, London, 1967). For an assessment of Walter Laqueur as a historian and contemporary witness, see Paul Lendvai, *Die verspielte Welt*, Salzburg, 2019, pp. 139–145.

16. Harold Laski, *Law and Justice in the Soviet Union*, London, 1935, p. 24.

17. This and the following quote come from Davies, *Als USA-Botschafter in Moskau*, p. 33.

18. The term "fifth column" comes from the Spanish Civil War and was used to describe supporters of the rebellious Franco nationalists; in general, it refers to groups suspected of subversion who collaborate with an enemy power.

19. Bernard Pares, *Russia*, London, 1940, quoted in Laqueur, *The Fate of the Revolution*, p. 24.

20. Laqueur, *The Fate of the Revolution*, p. 25.

21. Laqueur published a new revised edition of his book in 1987, entitled *The Fate of the Revolution: Interpretations of Soviet History from 1917 to the Present*.

22. *Foreign Affairs*, 15 April 1923.

23. See Vladimir Putin's State of the Nation Address of 25 April 2005.

3. GERMANY'S BLIND RUSSIA POLICY

1. Joachim Gauck and Helga Hirsch, *Erschütterungen: Was unsere Demokratie von außen und innen bedroht*, Munich, 2023.

2. See Lendvai, *Auf schwarzen Listen*, pp. 249–293.

3. For an assessment of Frank-Walter Steinmeier's behaviour, see the next chapter. On Heinz Fischer's statement that behaviour at any time should be assessed from the perspective of that time, see *Der Standard*, 8 March 2022.

4. Gauck and Hirsch, *Erschütterungen*, pp. 14–15.

5. *Süddeutsche Zeitung*, 2 and 8 September 2014.

6. "Europe's Mission", *Die Welt*, 1 September 2014.

7. Gauck and Hirsch, *Erschütterungen*, p. 20.

8. *Frankfurter Allgemeine Zeitung*, 11 May 2023.

9. *Taz*, 2 February 2023.

10. Most recently in the ARD programme *Hart aber fair*, 27 February 2023.

11. Interview with Angela Merkel in *Die Zeit*, 7 December 2022.

12. For this and the following statements, see Gauck and Hirsch, *Erschütterungen*, pp. 94–103.

13. Gauck and Hirsch, *Erschütterungen*, p. 101.

14. Gauck and Hirsch, *Erschütterungen*, p. 102.

15. *Die Zeit*, 26 March 2014.

16. *Bild*, 16 May 2014.

17. See Serhii Plokhy, *Das Tor Europas, Die Geschichte der Ukraine*, Hamburg, 2022; and *Der Angriff: Russlands Krieg gegen die Ukraine und seine Folgen für die Welt*, Hamburg, 2023.

18. Ernest Renan, "What Is a Nation?", lecture at the Sorbonne, 11 March 1882.

19. Jürgen Habermas, "Krieg und Empörung", *Süddeutsche Zeitung*, 28 April 2022.
20. This and the following quotes come from Jürgen Habermas, "A Plea for Negotiations", *Süddeutsche Zeitung*, 14 February 2023.
21. *Neue Zürcher Zeitung*, 23 February 2023.
22. According to change.org, the global platform for online petitions headquartered in San Francisco, 820,000 signatories had signed the petition by mid-June 2023.
23. *Süddeutsche Zeitung*, 23 February 2023. The reference to Richard David Precht and Harald Welzer is to their joint book, *Die vierte Gewalt*, Frankfurt, 2022, in which the two authors criticise what they see as the media's overly pro-Ukrainian reporting.
24. Süddeutsche Zeitung, 6 April 2023.
25. All quotes from *Osteuropa*, 72, nos. 9–10 (2022), pp. 245–265. Despite this damning study, their two Putin-friendly books were published in new editions with updated introductions in 2023.
26. Gauck and Hirsch, *Erschütterungen*, pp. 131–133.

4. FROM WILLY BRANDT TO GERHARD SCHRÖDER: THE SPLENDOUR AND MISERY OF SPD POLICY TOWARDS THE EAST

1. Bingener and Wehner, *Die Moskau-Connection*. See also S Dobert-U. Thiele, Nordstream-Wie Deutschland Putins Kreig bezahlt, Stuttgart 2025.
2. Paul Lendvai and Karl Heinz Ritschel, *Kreisky: Porträt eines Staatsmannes* [Kreisky: Portrait of a Statesman], Vienna, 1972, p. 105.

3. Lendvai, *Auf schwarzen Listen*.

4. Günter Guillaume, one of Willy Brandt's closest collaborators, was exposed as a GDR spy on 24 April 1974 and arrested; Willy Brandt subsequently resigned.

5. Heinrich August Winkler, "When the SPD Became Conservative", *Der Spiegel*, 12 June 2022.

6. Quoted from Bingener and Wehner, *Die Moskau-Connection*, p. 68.

7. *Die Zeit*, 10 November 2022.

8. *Frankfurter Allgemeine Zeitung*, 10 July 2023.

9. Bingener and Wehner, *Die Moskau-Connection*, pp. 70–71.

10. Klaus von Dohnanyi, *Nationale Interessen: Orientierung für deutsche und europäische Politik in Zeiten globaler Umbrüche* [National Interests: Orientation for German and European Politics in Times of Global Upheaval], Munich, 2022.

11. Gauck and Hirsch, *Erschütterungen*, pp. 108–109.

12. Speech by Lars Klingbeil at an SPD event on 18 October 2022, https://www.spd.de/fileadmin/Dokumente/Reden/20221018_Rede_LK.pdf.

13. *Süddeutsche Zeitung*, 7 April 2023.

14. Kurt Kister in *Süddeutsche Zeitung*, 9 February 2022.

15. Bingener and Wehner, *Die Moskau-Connection*, p. 275.

16. Bingener and Wehner, *Die Moskau-Connection*, p. 108.

17. Quoted from the ARD interview with Reinhold Beckmann, 23 November 2004.

18. Wolfram Weimer, N-TV, 26 April 2022; and *Süddeutsche Zeitung*, 9 February 2022.

19. Bingener and Wehner, *Die Moskau-Connection*, p. 189.

20. Stephan Weil, https://www.stephanweil.de/2020/09/07/sanktionen-sind-sackgassen/.

21. *Die Zeit*, 7 October 2020.
22. Quoted from *Die Zeit* (online), 28 January 2022.
23. Angela Merkel, *Freedom, 1954–2021*, London, 2024.
24. *Süddeutsche Zeitung*, 4 April 2022.

5. YUGOSLAV WARS: THE BITTER CONSEQUENCES OF IGNORANCE

1. Mappes-Niediek, *Krieg in Europa*, p. 358.
2. Paul Lendvai, *Der rote Balkan: Zwischen Nationalismus und Kommunismus*, Frankfurt am Main, 1969, p. 190.
3. Mappes-Niediek, *Krieg in Europa*, pp. 293–294.
4. For the best summaries, see Mappes-Niediek, *Krieg in Europa*; Holm Sundhaussen, *Geschichte Serbiens*, Vienna, 2007; Marie-Janine Calic, *Geschichte Jugoslawiens*, Munich, 2010.
5. Holm Sundhaussen, *Jugoslawien und seine Nachfolgestaaten, 1943–2011*, Vienna, 2012, p. 517.
6. Tom Gallagher, "Milošević, Serbia and the West during the Yugoslav Wars, 1991–1995", in Andrew Hammond (ed.), *The Balkans and the West*, Aldershot, 2004, pp. 157, 161.
7. Josip Glaurdić, *The Hour of Europe: Western Powers and the Breakup of Yugoslavia*, London, 2011, p. 1.
8. This and the following quote from Mappes-Niediek, *Krieg in Europa*, pp. 110–111.
9. Hans-Dietrich Genscher, *Erinnerungen* [Memoirs], Berlin, 1995, p. 966.
10. Richard Holbrooke, *Meine Mission: Vom Krieg zum Frieden in Bosnien* [My Mission: From War to Peace in Bosnia], Munich, 1998 (originally published in English as *To End a War*, New York, 1998).

11. Holbrooke, *Meine Mission*, p. 242.

12. George Packer, *Our Man: Richard Holbrooke and the End of the American Century*, New York, 2019.

13. Julien Benda, *La trahison des clercs*, quoted from Paul Lendvai, *Zwischen Hoffnung und Ernüchterung*, Vienna, 1994, pp. 216–217.

14. Mihailo Marković, in *Europäische Rundschau*, no. 1 (1975).

15. *The Economist*, 10 December 1993.

16. Bogdan Bogdanović, *Der verdammte Baumeister: Erinnerungen*, Vienna, 1997, pp. 262–264.

17. Sundhaussen, *Jugoslawien und seine Nachfolgestaaten*, p. 247.

18. "Zur Anatomie einer Revolution", *Europäische Rundschau*, no. 4 (2001). See also Paul Lendvai, *Reflexionen eines kritischen Europäers*, Vienna, 2005, pp. 99–120.

19. His trial began in February 2002 and ended without judgment with his death in March 2006. The tribunal sentenced Radovan Karadžić in 2019 and Ratko Mladić in 2021 to life imprisonment for genocide, war crimes and crimes against humanity.

20. Arnold J. Toynbee, *Erlebnisse und Erfahrungen* [Experiences], Munich, 1970, p. 50.

6. THE BALKANS: PLAYGROUND FOR WESTERN HYPOCRITES

1. Croatia was the last state to be admitted to the EU in 2013; Kosovo, independent since 2008, has applied for membership in 2022.

2. See Lendvai, *Die verspielte Welt*, pp. 53–64.

3. *Süddeutsche Zeitung*, 31 March 2023.

4. *Der Standard*, 16 October 2019.

5. Quoted from *Wiener Zeitung*, 11 April 2023.

6. *The Economist*, 7 November 2019.

7. Embassy of France in Washington, Closing speech by the President of the Republic at the Globsec Bratislava Forum, published on 2 June 2023, Deutsche Welle, 31 May 2023.

8. *Der Standard*, 17 July 2022.

9. *Frankfurter Allgemeine Zeitung*, 23 February 2022.

10. *Kurier*, 9 March 2023.

11. Adelheid Wölfl, *NZZ Magazine*, 11 June 2023.

12. *Neue Zürcher Zeitung*, 23 June 2023.

13. NATO soldiers have been stationed in Kosovo since 1999 (today only 4,500) to secure peace between Albanians and Serbs.

14. *Der Standard*, 1 August 2023.

15. *Der Standard*, 25 September 2023.

16. *Der Standard*, 2 October 2023; and *Neue Zürcher Zeitung*, 24 October 2023.

17. Press conference by Angela Merkel and Aleksandar Vučić at the Federal Chancellery on 27 February 2018.

18. Aleks Eror, "How Aleksandar Vučić Became Europe's Favourite Autocrat", *Foreign Policy*, 9 March 2018.

7. VIKTOR ORBÁN: THE WORLD CHAMPION OF CYNICISM

1. Bálint Magyar and Bálint Madlovics, "Kommentar der anderen", *Der Standard*, 25 June 2019.

2. Interview with Ágnes Heller in *Spiegel Online*, 12 April 2018. For the various definitions of the Orbán regime, see Paul Lendvai, *Orbáns Ungarn* [Orbán's Hungary], revised edition, Vienna, 2021, pp. 98 and 232. For comprehensive

descriptions, see also Zsuzsanna Szelényi, *Tainted Democracy: Viktor Orbán and the Subversion of Hungary*, London 2023; Pál Dániel Rényi, *Győzelmi kényszer: Futball és hatalom Orbán világában* [The Compulsion to Win: Football and Power in Orbán's World], Budapest, 2021; Stefano Bottoni, *A hatalom megszállottja: Orbán Viktor Magyarországa* [Obsessed with Power: Viktor Orbán's Hungary], Budapest, 2023; Melani Barlai, Florian Hartleb and Dániel Mikecz, *Das politische System Ungarns* [The Hungarian Political System], Baden-Baden, 2023.

3. Gábor Fodor and four other MPs left Fidesz in November 1993 and later joined the liberal SzDSz.

4. Paul Lendvai, "Im Brennpunkt Spezial: Genies, Verlierer, Lebenskünstler—Ungarn", ORF documentary, broadcast on 1 October 1999.

5. For details, see Lendvai, *Orbáns Ungarn*, pp. 89–90.

6. Gideon Rachman, *Welt der Autokraten* [World of Autocrats], Berlin, 2022, p. 143 (published in English as *The Age of the Strongman*, London, 2022).

7. *Der Standard*, 22 September 2010; see also Lendvai, *Orbáns Ungarn*, pp. 117–133.

8. Lendvai, *Orbáns Ungarn*, p. 120.

9. Speech by Viktor Orbán on 26 July 2014 in Băile Tuşnad; see also Lendvai, *Orbáns Ungarn*, p. 225.

10. Hungarian news agency MTI, 11 January 2015.

11. *European Review*, no. 1 (2016).

12. See also Lendvai, *Orbáns Ungarn*, p. 123.

13. On the international campaign against George Soros, see the next chapter.

14. *Der Standard*, 15 September 2022.

15. Viktor Orbán, State of the Nation Address, Budapest, 16 February 2020.

16. Bottoni, *A hatalom megszállottja*, pp. 174–176.

17. *Süddeutsche Zeitung*, 22 October 2023.

18. Mariam Lau, "Die Orbanologie", *Die Zeit*, 22 December 2022; Stephan Löwenstein, "Orbáns Elitenschmiede", *Frankfurter Allgemeine Zeitung*, 3 August 2023.

19. *Die Zeit*, 6 July 2023.

20. All quotes in this paragraph from *Die Zeit*, 6 July 2023.

8. GEORGE SOROS: FROM ADMIRED PHILANTHROPIST TO HATED DEMON

1. Lendvai, *Die verspielte Welt*, pp. 171–187; and Lendvai, *Orbáns Ungarn*, pp. 218–222.

2. Soros studied under the Viennese-born philosopher Karl Popper, who had written his magnum opus *The Open Society and Its Enemies* in English in New Zealand during the Second World War. The book was published in London in 1945.

3. Most recently in German: George Soros, *Für die Verteidigung der offenen Gesellschaft*, Kulmbach, 2019. See also the anthology *George Soros: A Life in Full*, edited by Peter L. W. Osnos, Boston, 2022.

4. *New Yorker*, 15 January 1995.

5. Bottoni, *A hatalom megszállottja*, pp. 25–27.

6. George Soros, "The CEU and Its Future", in *In Defence of the Open Society*, New York, 2019, pp. 89–104.

7. *Élet és Irodalom*, 14 August 2020.

8. *Heti Világgazdaság* (*HVG*), 15 June 2017.

9. *Das Magazin*, weekend supplement of the *Tagesanzeiger*, 12 January 2019.

10. For his role, see Lendvai, *Orbáns Ungarn*, pp. 164–165.

11. *Frankfurter Allgemeine Zeitung*, 19 July 2018.

12. *HVG*, 4 May 2023.
13. At the end of 2021, the Russian Supreme Court banned the entire Memorial organisation.
14. *New York Times*, 11 October 2019.
15. *Süddeutsche Zeitung*, 31 March 2023.
16. *Forbes*, 16 May 2023.
17. Peter Frank, "Dauermobilisierung in Ungarn", *Osteuropa*, 68, nos. 3–5 (2018), pp. 33–55; see also Lendvai, *Die verspielte Welt*, pp. 180–181.
18. Rachman, *Welt der Autokraten*, p. 288.
19. Franz Schuh, *Vom Guten, Wahren und Schlechten: Ein Lesebuch*, Vienna, 2022, p. 336.

9. SEBASTIAN KURZ: THE MAN BEHIND THE MASKS

1. The co-defendants were Bernhard Bonelli, head of cabinet in the Federal Chancellery under Sebastian Kurz, and his successor, Alexander Schallenberg, and the former ÖVP deputy party leader Bettina Glatz-Kremsner, CEO of Casinos Austria and chairwoman of the Management Board of Austrian Lotteries until March 2022. Bonelli was convicted and given a six-month suspended sentence, which was upheld in the May 2025 ruling. The proceedings against Glatz-Kremsner were dropped on the first day of the trial due to diversion; she must pay a fine of 104,000 euros.
2. See Paul Lendvai, *Vielgeprüftes Österreich* [Sorely Tried Austria], Salzburg, 2022, pp. 192–215.
3. *Die Zeit*, Austrian edition, 31 August 2023.
4. *Kronen Zeitung*, 17 September 2023.
5. Balázs Orbán, *The Hungarian Way of Strategy*, Budapest, 2021.

6. Fritz Hausjell, "Kommentar der anderen", *Der Standard*, 9 September 2023.

7. Interview in the Zagreb news portal *Tportal*, 4 June 2016.

8. *Der Spiegel*, 9 September 2019.

9. Armin Thurnher, *Anstandslos: Demokratie, Oligarchie, österreichische Abwege*, Vienna, 2023, p. 26.

10. *Wiener Zeitung*, 12 May 2017.

11. *Falter*, no. 49 (2021).

12. Sebastian Kurz with Conny Bischofberger, *Reden wir über Politik*, Vienna, 2022, p. 155.

13. Konrad Paul Liessmann, interview with the *Neue Zürcher Zeitung*, 17 January 2022.

14. Deutsche Welle, 7 October 2021.

15. *New York Times*, 12 August 2023.

16. Kurz with Bischofberger, *Reden wir über Politik*, p. 220.

17. Interview with Sebastian Kurz, *Kurier*, 12 March 2023.

18. *Kurier*, 17 June 2023.

19. According to the balance sheet, his company reported a profit of 1.9 million euros in 2022. *Heute* and *OE24*, 13 October 2023. See for increased profit Kleine Zeitung, October 15, 2025, for estimate of "Dream" *The Standard*, February 17, 2025.

20. *Capital*, German weekly, 25 February 2025.

21. *Bild*, 5 October 2023.

22. *Der Standard*, 22 August 2023.

23. Paul Ronzheimer, *Sebastian Kurz: Die Biografie*, Freiburg im Breisgrau, 2018, p. 121.

24. Ronzheimer, *Sebastian Kurz*, p. 181.

25. *Die Presse*, 17 December 2022.

INDEX OF NAMES